The Recollected Heart

A Monastic

Retreat with

Philip Zaleski

THE
RECOLLECTED
HEART

Philip Zaleski

HarperSanFrancisco
A Division of HarperCollins*Publishers*

THE RECOLLECTED HEART: *A Monastic
Retreat with Philip Zaleski.* Copyright ©
1995 by Philip Zaleski. All rights reserved.
Printed in the United States of America.
No part of this book may be used or repro-
duced in any manner whatsoever without
written permission except in the case of
brief quotations embodied in critical articles
and reviews. For information address
HarperCollins Publishers, 10 East 53rd
Street, New York, NY 10022.

HarperCollins,® 🏢®, and
HarperSanFrancisco™ are trademarks of
HarperCollins Publishers Inc.

Illustrations by Kathleen Edwards
Book design by Ralph Fowler
Set in Granjon

FIRST HARPERCOLLINS PAPERBACK
EDITION PUBLISHED IN 1995

Library of Congress
Cataloging-in-Publication Data

Zaleski, Philip.
The recollected heart : a monastic retreat with
Philip Zaleski / Philip Zaleski.
p. cm.
ISBN: 0-06-069781-4 (pbk.)
1. Retreats. 2. Zaleski, Philip. I. Title
BX2375.A3Z35 1995
269'.6—dc20   95-9272

95 96 97 98 99 ❖HAD 10 9 8 7 6 5 4 3 2 1

to Carol

Contents

Acknowledgments

My warmest thanks go to the Benedictine monks and nuns of Petersham, Massachusetts, without whom this book would have been impossible. I owe a particular debt to Rev. Dom Anselm Atkinson, O.S.B., Superior of St. Mary's Monastery, and to the Very Rev. Mother Mary Clare Vincent, O.S.B., Prioress of St. Scholastic Priory. St. Benedict must be smiling in heaven at the sight of his monasteries in such capable hands.

I wish to express my gratitude to the many people who helped me in one way or another in the preparation of this book, including Stratford and Léonie Caldecott; Rt. Rev. Dom Hugh Gilbert, O.S.B., Abbot of Pluscarden Abbey; Rev. Dom Bede Kierney, O.S.B.; Susan Anderson Kerr; Jean Sulzberger; Rev. David Turner, O.S.B.; and the many members of the western Massachusetts contemplative prayer group. Thanks also to Annie Dillard for suggesting me for this project; to my editor, Kandace Hawkinson, and her assistant, Erica Smith, for their unstinting support; and to my family for giving me the best reason in the world to come back from retreat.

A Note on Translations

Most biblical quotations in the text come from the New Revised Standard Version Bible (copyright 1989, Division of Christian Education of the National Council of the Churches of Christ in the United States of America). However, now and then I have turned to other translations in order to highlight the traditional meaning of a particular teaching or event. These translations include the Revised Standard Version Bible (copyright 1946, 1952, 1971, Division of Christian Education of the National Council of the Churches of Christ in the United States of America) and the King James Version Bible. All such instances are noted in the text.

All quotations from St. Benedict's *Rule* come from *RB 1980: The Rule of St. Benedict in Latin and English with Notes* (Collegeville, MN: Liturgical Press, 1981). The translation from Dante's *Paradiso* in chapter 5 was prepared by my wife, Carol Zaleski.

Part One

SOURCES

Come away by
yourselves to a
lonely place, and
rest a while.

—Mark 6:31

Chapter One

THE
NATURE
OF
RETREAT

S everal years ago, I found myself in the strange and comical situation, as the ancient Middle Eastern saying has it, of "trying to jump over my own knees." A major decision loomed, one whose consequences would shake every pillar of my life. I fretted over my possibilities, I fiddled and fussed. Try as I might, I couldn't make a final choice. Alternatives A, C, E, and G pointed to failure, along a spectrum ranging from discomfort to catastrophe. Plans B, D, and F promised success, but they entailed sacrifices that I felt unwilling to make. I was bewildered, half-beaten, queasy in my soul. Well-meaning friends gave me conflicting advice: to leap forward, to back-paddle, to give up. Books proved to be another dead end: The first steered me north; the next, due south. What to do?

To break the stalemate, I went on retreat. I borrowed a friend's cabin up in the New Hampshire woods, a rustic affair at the end of an unmarked dirt road, with night crawlers in the basement and bats in the attic. The nearest neighbors ran a small dairy farm a half mile to the south. To the north rose the rocky face of Mt. Washington, New England's tallest peak, where a few decades ago meteorologists had measured the strongest winds on record, whipping the weather vanes at 231 miles per hour. Although I never climbed the mountain, for the span of my exile I felt like I was standing on the summit, with those hurricane winds roaring through my soul. For five days I was cut off, cut loose, I was *away:* atop the world, light-years from Earth, gazing back like some distant astronaut on our little green-and-blue ball of life. Blessed Julian of Norwich's vision flashed into my mind, of the time that God had presented her with the world:

> He showed me something small, no bigger than a hazelnut, lying in the palm of my hand, and I perceived that it was as round as any ball. I looked at it and thought: What can this be? And I was given this general answer: It is everything which is made. I was amazed that it could last, for I thought that it was so little that it could suddenly fall into nothing. And I was answered in my understanding: It lasts and always will, because God loves it; and thus everything has being through the love of God.[1]

Ralph Waldo Emerson had a similar experience:

> I dreamed that I floated at will in the great Ether, and I saw this world floating also not far off, but diminished to the size of an apple. Then an angel took it in his hand and brought it to me and said, "This must thou eat." And I ate the world.

Visionary nuns and dreaming poets: What better guides than these for my retreat? Reason had failed to answer my dilemma; perhaps in vapors and chimeras I would find what I sought. But I wasn't ready just yet to eat the world. Rather, I was savoring abstinence, this sudden escape from my regular feast of gossip and "news." No newspapers, magazines, or TV broadcasts intruded during those few days of retreat. And this privation—which from the first I knew would be a blessing— proved to be only the beginning. A deeper solitude was mine.

No human beings crossed my path—no inquisitive neighbors, no friends who "just heard I was alone and stopped by to make sure that I was okay." No letters, telegrams, or phone calls invaded my mountain aerie. No one knew where I was; I might have been on Mars. I tipped my cap to grazing sheep on my early morning stroll and accepted a nuzzle from my neighbor's cow on my after-dinner constitutional. Apart from these happy salutations, I was utterly alone.

Soon after arriving at my country cabin, I sat down to smoke a pipeful of cherry tobacco (today I'd be content to chew a wad of gum) and contemplate the pinkish gray clouds curling around the Presidential peaks. I felt as snug as Robinson Crusoe tucked away in his island safehold, and half-imagined grabbing flintlock and umbrella for a pleasant stroll along the beach. As the sky-wisps cleaved and coagulated overhead, memories flooded back of earlier times when I had gone off to be alone. I realized that retreat—this need to be with myself for a time, to make a little world within the world where I could be safe, and where I could think—was a leitmotiv of my life. And so it is with everyone. We all enter the world after a good retreat, nine months in our mother's womb, in the cushioned serenity of the amniotic ocean, where the miraculous transformation from one level of being to another takes place, and a clump of cells becomes a bawling baby. A comparable transformation, it struck me, is what we adults seek when we make for the hills. We seek rebirth, in things large and small. We long to be refreshed, reseeded, reinspired, to "be renewed in the spirit," as St. Paul puts it so stirringly in his letter to the Ephesians.

As the clouds swirled, so did my mind, and memories of earlier retreats rose to consciousness. I remembered Boy Scout camp, at the age of nine or ten. This summer holiday proved to be a retreat within a retreat, for the camp, pocketed deep in the woods and thus an exile from my ordinary suburban life, disclosed itself to me as a frightening place where I, a shy, bookish boy more comfortable pitching an idea than a tent, knew hardly a soul and couldn't grasp the rules. So I wrangled my way into the job of troop mail boy and spent a good chunk of each day walking at a turtle's pace to the post office, several miles away from our encampment, a heavenly excursion in which I could simply be myself and confront nothing more threatening that a lost backpacker or a lumbering porcupine. In this escape from camp—itself an escape from ordinary life—I first tasted the terror and bliss of solitude.

I recalled, too, times at college when I would leave my partying roommates in the smoky common room, plunge into the cold night air, and make for the hidden garden tucked behind one of the Greek Revival mansions that dotted the campus, there to prop my back against a concrete birdbath, breathe deeply, and pray. Other self-imposed enclosures came back: winter in a Vermont cabin, spring in an Istanbul hotel, summer in a Wyoming lodge, autumn in a Parisian apartment; retreats before births and after deaths, retreats during times of crisis and times of peace. These many periods of self-renewal taught me what to expect this time, snuggled at the foot of the New Hampshire mountains. Certain things always happen on retreat—at least, if one is properly prepared. Time slows down, space dilates. Objects attain a starkness of outline and brilliancy of color that they rarely possess in ordinary life. Things become transparent, and their essential being shines through. While on retreat, I find that when I lift a fork, I register its well-balanced weight, the elegance of its four-tined design, just right for the task at hand (three may not hold a slippery morsel; five would be excessive). When I chew a raspberry, its flavor explodes in my mouth. The whole fruit rushes forth to meet me: the tiny hairs stubbling the skin, the tart juice, the rough globular joy of its raspberriness, like a red sun come down to earth.

I, too, change while on retreat. As the world comes to me, I go forth to greet it, gladly. I slow down, take my time with things, enter into each activity with all my being. When I sit, I really sit, and my weight settles into the earth. When I stand, my legs become pillars, supporting the great trunk of spine and chest, the architectonic wizardry of arms, neck, and head. When I walk, I feel the frigid air pumping into my lungs; I sense against my palms the dry scratch of woolen gloves; I hear, as a definite fracture in the fabric of silence, the crack and snap of branches breaking underfoot. Such events shed their remoteness, their alienness. They speak to me, friend to friend, and I begin to listen.

But all this is the least of it. Away from the world's ceaseless din, one hears whispers from another realm, faint but compelling. Honed senses, vitality, other external changes—as valuable as they may be—only hint at the real transformation to be found. New possibilities beckon, fresh ways of seeing, doing, and being, priceless gifts at once familiar and strange. One is *perspective;* another is *prayer.*

We all know what perspective means (but how rarely we attain it): the ability to see a situation objectively, as someone else might see it. Its importance cannot be overstated. The hunt for perspective explains not only why we go on weekend retreat, but why people set off for distant continents, why athletes have coaches, writers have editors, and everyone (even God, insists the Christian tradition) has a mother. On retreat we see with new eyes, we think with new minds. We become our own counselors, and sometimes we even take our own good advice.

Even more important, however, is the advent of prayer. I use the term "advent" (which means "coming" or "arrival") deliberately. For each time we pray, it is like coming up to another level of being, like swimming from stygian depths to the sunlit surface of a pool, where we float for a while in the presence of God. During my stay in the New Hampshire woods, I swam repeatedly upward, greeted the Sun that burns both day and night, and laid my burden in its scorching rays. I entrusted everything, once and for all, to God. I had little in the way of theology or metaphysics to guide me; I only knew that I needed a helpmeet infinitely more wise and ancient than myself. How to act? Where to turn? I did the only thing I could do: I fell to my knees and prayed.

To attain perspective and to pray—to become self-reliant by relying on God—this is no small ambition. Many learned tomes discuss the hows and whys, and none of them, I think, get it exactly right. I know that I didn't. Sometimes during my alpine retreat, I felt dizzy, in despair, on the verge of crumpling. At other times, I enjoyed the cool energies that quiet brings. For a while my plans would run smoothly, and then they would rupture beyond hope. But slowly, the fog of my confusion began to lift. In time an answer came. It always does, if one waits long enough and gives stillness, silence, and solitude a chance to do their work. Was I sure about my choice? No, not at all, but as G. K. Chesterton said, "If a thing is worth doing, it is worth doing badly." Chesterton, a man whose penetration into the human soul was as acute as his sense of paradox, also remarked, "I do not believe in a fate that falls on men however they act; but I do believe in a fate that falls on men unless they act." I acted; my life changed forever; I have had no regrets.

———————

"Society is like the air," wrote the American philosopher George Santayana, "Necessary to breathe, but insufficient to live on." To find real sustenance, as I discovered on that mountainside more than a decade ago, we must at times seek a place apart. The wish to retreat from the daily bump and bustle has given rise to many great spiritual adventures, unfolding in caves, on mountaintops, or in a quiet corner of a busy home. One thinks of Gautama Buddha meditating under the bodhi tree, or St. Simeon Stylites preaching on his desert pillar; for an example closer to our own day, one might picture Henry Thoreau anointing himself "inspector of snowdrifts" in the woods of Walden Pond, Admiral Richard Byrd shivering in the Antarctic interior (and reading *Walden* with relish as the blizzards howled), or Annie Dillard dazzled by the rippling of light along the banks of Tinker Creek.

Retreat, as all these seekers testify, is a richly textured affair, harboring something of exploration, something of escape, and something of life-and-death struggle. Whatever the mix, one truth abides: retreat is neither whim nor luxury nor self-indulgence, but a rock-bottom staple of a healthy life. We need retreat as surely as we need oxygen or protein. While any given retreat may start out as a joyride—a few days away from spouse, kids, or job, a chance at last to spread one's wings, loosen one's belt, kick up one's heels—it always winds up as a pilgrimage. We start to look for what really counts. Thoreau states the case unconditionally in this justly famous passage from *Walden*:

> I went to the woods because I wished to live deliberately, to front only the essential facts of life, and see if I could not learn what it had to teach, and not, when I came to die, discover that I had not lived. I did not wish to live what was not life, living is so dear, nor did I wish to practice resignation, unless it was quite necessary. I wanted to live deep and suck out all the marrow of life . . .

Retreat, then, is life stripped bare, boiled to the bones, pared to first and final things. In the Christian tradition, such uncloaking of self and senses plays an indispensable role in spiritual growth. God calls us, always and everywhere; our task is to find conditions that allow us to hear and respond to the divine invitation. Breaking from habit, filtering out the noise of the world, seeking a place apart: These are good ways to begin. But during the silence that follows, where will we incline our ears? Inward, answers Jesus, for "the kingdom of God is within you" (Luke 17:21, KJV). While philosophers have cracked their heads over the nuances of this statement, few people miss its central message: We must, as St. Augustine put it, "return to the heart" (the spiritual center, our true self) and there seek God. The earliest Christians call this process "recollection," the act of remembering (re-membering, re-collecting) ourselves, God, and the love that binds us. "Run away, be still, maintain recollection," counseled the fourth-century desert saint Abba Arsenius. During retreat, we stitch together, with the needle of silence and the thread of stillness, our scattered sense of self and our fragmentary experience of God.

To some, this process, with its emphasis on interior work, may sound like narcissism in the raw. Nothing could be further from the truth. Jesus' proclamation that "the kingdom of God is within you" can also be correctly translated as "the kingdom of God is among you"—that is, in the collectivity of all human beings. Turning inward means turning outward (the spiritual life teems with such happy paradoxes). Jesus, while proclaiming through word and deed the absolute necessity for periodic retreat, nonetheless engaged in an active ministry of preaching, healing, and prophecy. Like Jesus, we too may find that retreat leads to total engagement with others. This curious motion—simultaneously inward and outward, toward myself and toward the world—lies at the heart of this simple Danish folk tale, relayed by Søren Kierkegaard:

> A man . . . was so tired of his home that he had his horse saddled
> in order to ride forth into the wide world. When he had gone a
> little distance his horse threw him. This turn of events was deci-

sive for him, for when he turned to mount his horse his eye lit again upon the home he wished to leave, and he looked, and behold! it was so beautiful that he at once turned back.[2]

By going on retreat, we give ourselves the opportunity—without, one hopes, too severe a bump—to dismount, turn around, and see our life afresh. At its very best, this vision brings with it joy, energy, and a sense of purpose that revitalizes us and, inevitably, those around us. It may even change the world. Perhaps you remember when Jimmy Carter, Anwar Sadat, and Menachem Begin, devout men from different faiths, met together at Camp David in a week-long huddle, often punctuated by prayer, that the participants pointedly called a "retreat" and that gave birth to the Arab-Israeli peace accord. Can you imagine such a splendid result, of benefit to all humankind, resulting from secular, public talks in Geneva or Stockholm? So may it fare with our own spiritual retreats: In ways beyond measure and times beyond counting, may they bear fruit in the world.

The Camp David event tells us something else important about retreat: We needn't insist upon forty days in the wilderness. Even a three-day withdrawal from ordinary life permits serious spiritual work to begin. By the third day, our exile can become a cosmos unto itself, where we may, if we open ourselves unreservedly to God, encounter truths that evade us in the haste and heat of ordinary life. The same flexibility applies to our choice of locale. Admiral Byrd's subterranean polar hut has its charms, including total solitude, security, and a symbolic affinity to the womb. Some Tibetan Buddhists go so far as to immure themselves within a cave for life, with only a narrow slit remaining unsealed to allow the passage of food, water, and wastes. However, for our purposes a house, apartment, cabin, tent, or monastic guest room will do just as well. I once knew a man who made an annual retreat in the Maine woods with nothing but a blanket, a book, and a background knowledge of local herbs and berries. The essential thing is to divorce ourselves, as far as possible, from the habits and pressures of our workaday lives. If we drag our old patterns into the retreat, we will soil our surroundings and spoil our chances for a vital encounter with God. Some Native Americans parboil in a sweat lodge before undertaking a vision quest or other sacred activity that entails withdrawal from the world. On our retreat, the same principle holds: We must wash away the old world before entering the new (this process will be discussed in more detail in chapter 3). Such inner ablutions aside, there remains only one prerequisite for our retreat: a genuine desire to bathe in the abyss of God's love. If we settle for dipping our toes, we may enjoy a pleasant vacation from ordinary life, even bring back some picturesque snapshots of our time apart, but we can be certain that little wisdom will come our way. If we dive in boldly, however, if we take the plunge with all our being, we will swim the depths that, like the waters of fable, may renew our lives.

———————

The roots of Christian retreat burrow into antiquity, to the primordial retreats of Moses in the Sinai wilderness. According to the Book of Exodus, Moses' first withdrawal from the world—and his first encounter with God—came unexpectedly, while he tended his sheep on Mt. Horeb. An "angel of the Lord" appeared in the form of a burning bush, a plant that never turned to charcoal, for it blazed with a spiritual flame. Speaking through the bush, God revealed to Moses the Divine Name, placed on his shoulders the mantle of prophecy, and promised to the Israelites deliverance from slavery. Years later, Moses again scaled the Sinai heights—this time on deliberate retreat—there to receive the Ten Commandments, along with instructions for erecting the sacred tabernacle and the Ark of the Covenant.

What can we glean from these mountain ascents of Moses, which showered such an abundance of gifts upon the world? Perfect prototypes, they display the quintessential elements of all retreat:

> *Retreat leads to divine gifts.* During his withdrawal from the world, Moses—who here represents all human beings—opens his heart to God, and God in turn grants to Moses and his people all that they desire: a teacher, a moral code, a ritual practice, a land in which to thrive. "Take delight in the Lord, and he will give you the desires of your heart," exclaims the Hebrew Psalter (Psalm 37:4).

> *Retreat never takes place alone.* Once Moses scales the mountain, God never abandons him. So it is with us on our retreat: We will never be alone. Tradition assures us, on the contrary, that throughout our lives—and most emphatically while on retreat—God mantles us with love, the air throngs with angels, and saints kindly bend their heads our way.

> *Retreat demands special conditions and behavior.* During Moses' first ascent, a voice commands him to "remove the sandals from your feet, for the place on which you are standing is holy ground" (Exodus 3:5; the ground is hallowed, of course, by God's presence). As we climb our own Sinai, we too will need to take appropriate measures, symbolically removing the sandals from our feet.

According to Christian tradition, the great retreats of Moses and other Hebrew prophets—Abraham, Isaac, Jacob, so many generations of seers that they make the head spin—lead in "the fullness of time" to those undertaken by God incarnate,

Jesus Christ. The New Testament abounds with references to Jesus' retreats, and to his counsels on the subject: Jesus "got up and went out to a deserted place, and there he prayed" (Mark 1:35); Jesus instructs his disciples to "come away to a deserted place all by yourselves and rest a while" (Mark 6:31); Jesus tells us, in the Sermon on the Mount, "Whenever you pray, go into your room and shut the door and pray to your Father who is in secret" (Matthew 6:5).

These varied prescriptions come to fruition in Jesus' withdrawal into the desert immediately following his baptism: "Jesus, full of the Holy Spirit, returned from the Jordan and was led by the Spirit in the wilderness" (Luke 4:1–2). Here, alone for forty days, he engaged in spiritual combat, described by Luke in mythological terms involving three temptations by the devil: to change stone into bread, to rule the earth, and to plummet from a mountain and be saved by angels. Jesus resists these trials, prototypes of all the difficulties which we encounter on the spiritual path (the temptations of indulgence, power, and pride, respectively).

Upon his return, Jesus reads the following messianic passage from Isaiah in the synagogue at Nazareth:

> The Spirit of the Lord is upon me, because he has anointed me to bring good news to the poor. He has sent me to proclaim release to the captives and recovery of sight to the blind, to let the oppressed go free, to proclaim the year of the Lord's favor.
> *(Luke 4:18–19)*

Through this proclamation, Jesus declares his own assumption of the messianic office. Despite the uniqueness of his role, his words—in a lesser key, of course—may speak for us as well. We too seek, in our own way, "the Spirit of the Lord" on our retreat; we too, upon our return, may have "good news" to convey.

In time, the retreats of Moses and Jesus became paradigms for the disciplines of Western monasticism. Centers of religious formation sprang up—first in Egypt and Syria, then in Europe, and eventually in Asia and the Americas—that bore fruit in extraordinary ventures in spiritual transformation. Consider, for example, the fourth-century retreat of St. Antony of the Desert, the prototypical Christian monk, who secreted himself inside a ruined fortress for—incredibly—twenty years. The following passage, from *The Life of Antony* by St. Athanasius, describes the saint emerging from his solitude:

> The state of his soul was one of purity, for it was not constricted by grief, nor relaxed by pleasure, nor affected by either laughter or dejection. Moreover, when he saw the crowd, he was not annoyed any more than he was elated at being embraced by so many people. He maintained utter equilibrium, like one guided by reason and steadfast in that which accords with nature. Through him the Lord healed many of those present who suffered from bodily ailments. . . . he consoled many who mourned, and others hostile to each other he reconciled in friendship.[3]

In his courage, compassion, and serenity, Antony serves as a model for all who seek the treasures of the heart. Over the centuries, innumerable men and women have followed his example—usually without becoming cave-bound hermits for twenty years. For a more typical form of Christian retreat, we might consider the example set by Augustine, who shortly after his conversion in 387 sequestered himself with his mother, St. Monica, in a comfortable house at Ostia at the mouth of the Tiber River. There, he writes, "our conversation was serene and joyful." Augustine goes on to offer a radiant description of the blessings of spiritual retreat, this time enjoyed by two people in unison (in the following passage from the *Confessions*, the "you" is God; with characteristic audacity, Augustine addressed this glorious book, the world's first autobiography and still the best, directly to his Maker):

> As the flame of love burned stronger in us and raised us higher toward the eternal God, our thoughts ranged over the whole compass of material things in their various degrees, up to the heavens themselves, from which the sun and the moon and the stars shine down upon the earth. Higher still we climbed, thinking and speaking all the while in wonder at all that you have made. . . . And while we spoke of the eternal Wisdom, longing for it and straining for it with all the strength of our hearts, for one fleeting instant we reached out and touched it.[4]

Not all retreats take place under such sunny conditions, however, or result in such graceful understandings. For a radical contrast in circumstance, let us leap forward a brace of centuries to the imprisonments of St. John of the Cross (1542–91) and John Bunyan (1628–88). In both cases, years in solitary confinement—involuntary retreat, one is tempted to call it, while wincing at the impertinence—led to profound spiritual insights and, not incidentally, to some of the world's great religious literature (from John of the Cross, a wealth of prose and poetry including *The Ascent of Mt. Carmel;* from Bunyan, *The Pilgrim's Progress*). For another contrast, consider St. Catherine of Siena (1347–80), who spent three teenage years in almost total solitude, a fierce discipline that led to a "mystical marriage to Christ" as well as her most important book, *The Dialogue,* which takes Augustine's literary temerity one step further, for in it God addresses the reader in the first person. Nor do idiosyncratic Christian retreats grind to a halt in modern times; one thinks of John Henry Newman's exile from Oxford University to the stables of Littlemore in 1842, or C. S. Lewis's walking tours of rural England, or Annie Dillard's retreat to the hinterlands of Virginia just a few decades ago.

These many examples underscore the diversity of retreat. Jesus slept in the open air, Antony a rotting garrison, Newman a stable, Dillard a creekside cabin. While Augustine and his mother shared a roof, most retreatants choose to be alone. Often, however, these preferences come to naught: Many solitaries—Newman and Antony, for instance—soon attract fellow seekers who bunk down alongside them willy-nilly. Some retreats precede great events, as an anticipatory gathering of spiritual energies, while others come as an aftermath, a chance to reflect after the dust has settled. Just as retreats vary in form or style, so they vary in content. We can never anticipate what will happen. Our time apart may overturn a lifetime of convictions or confirm our fondest beliefs. Whatever our experiences, we do well to keep in mind the grand procession of men and women who have proceeded us. The moment that we decide to withdraw from the world, however brief our retreat, however hesitant our resolve, we forge a new link in a great chain of retreatants stretching back across millennia to the ancient Israelites; we join in a common enterprise with Moses and all his spiritual progeny. Once again, the truth obtains: On retreat, we are never alone.

Chapter Two

THE
MONASTIC
MATRIX

The little chapel sleeps. Sunlight floods the interior, pouring through the floor-to-ceiling glass windows. Sitting in the pews and looking out, one sees a stone statue of the Blessed Virgin Mary, a faint smile on her face: in winter, Our Lady of the Snows, a frosty white bonnet on her cold head; in summer, Our Lady of the Flowers, encircled by a multicolored sea of blossoms. Inside the chapel, silence reigns. A scattering of people dot the pews, kneeling or sitting. Occasionally, one turns a page in a prayer book, making a thin, dry rustling that echoes against the whitewashed walls. Otherwise, all is stillness. The room waits.

Then comes change, infinitesimal at first, a slight trembling in the quality of the silence. The air shimmers with anticipation. The tread of feet can be heard far in the distance, growing stronger as it nears. The congregation waits. Suddenly a wave of black surges into the room, a great ebony crest of water, or so it seems at first. But this is a human current, a line of women dressed in black, black veils on black robes, black books in hand, so much black against the white sun-splashed walls that it dazzles the eye. The women flow into the chapel, two abreast, and the people in the pews rise: One cannot possibly sit through an event like this, which feels a bit like a parade, a bit like a funeral, and a lot like a royal procession. Then the nuns break into song, and it is as if heaven itself has thrown open its shutters to let the music out. The Gregorian chant lilts and purls, soars and tumbles like a bird coasting on the winds of God. As the nuns approach the altar, they bow two by two, turn left, and file into their choir stalls. Just then, as the high trill of the female voices thrills the spine, a deeper, rolling note sounds. Behind the nuns emerge larger forms, also garbed in black, without veils, but bearded: The monks have entered. They too bow toward the altar—making, like the nuns, a full bend from the waist, head dipping as low as possible—then turn right and process to their respective stalls. Now nuns and monks face one another, voices merged in song. Chant bathes the chapel, soaks the walls, saturates the pews. The Mass has begun.

This scene repeats itself every day of the year in Petersham, Massachusetts, at the Benedictine Monastic Center, home of the twin communities of St. Scholastica Priory, for women, and St. Mary's Monastery, for men. My wife and I visit the center with our eight-year-old son, John, whenever we can, to dip our souls in this holy atmosphere. Here live some of the happiest human beings I know. These monks and nuns suffer the same agonies as other people: rejection, frustration, fear, and so on. But underneath it all runs a current of pure joy, like a cold mountain river surging beneath a dusty city, and everyone senses its presence.

Here, I have often gone on retreat. I stay in the section of the guest house allotted to St. Mary's Monastery, dropping my bags in a small room containing nothing but a spartan bed, a battered table and chair, and a crucifix on the wall. I spend hours nestled in this room. Here I read, sleep, pray, meditate, fret, rejoice, simply spend time alone with God. I eat with the monks, take part in the liturgy, wander in the woods. But always I come back to this room. The first time I saw its four bare walls, I was terrified. What should I expect? How should I behave? Was I properly prepared? *What was I doing here?*

I needn't have worried. As I might have guessed, I was in capable hands. The monks and nuns assuaged my worries, broke through my stupidities, and taught me, mostly by example, a little bit about what retreat can be. It confirmed my intuition that in matters of the spirit, we do well to rely on experienced guides, those who have surveyed the peaks and valleys before us and can navigate the landscape blindfolded if need be. In many religions (Christianity, Buddhism, Hinduism most notably), such expertise concentrates in monasteries, amongst monks and nuns, men and women who have devoted their adult lives to the spiritual search. But I've discovered also that one needn't be on site to taste the fruits of the monastic way. Christian monastic practices adapt themselves readily to a retreat taken by oneself or with others beyond the monastery walls. Some share in the wisdom of nuns and monks can be ours as well, no matter where, when, or under what conditions we choose to go on retreat.

This chapter is entitled "The Monastic Matrix," and those with a taste for etymology will recognize matrix as a late Latin word meaning "womb," from the classical Latin *mater,* or "mother." Over the years, many ordinary people have found monasticism to be just that: mother to spiritual work of every kind and degree. One reason that monastic practices have proven so fertile is their simplicity. As we will see, they draw on the plainest, most common activities—sitting, singing, raking, reading—and transform each into a spiritual discipline of exquisite beauty and unsurpassed depth. Every aspect of our three-day retreat, from general comportment to specific prayers, springs from the womb of Western monasticism. Modifications have been introduced where necessary, but the monastic inspiration remains.

————————

Most Christian monasteries adhere to the *Rule* of St. Benedict; that is to say, they follow basic precepts of the monastic life first set down by St. Benedict of Nursia in the Italian hills some 1,500 years ago. Nearly two millennia later, Benedictinism remains the most widespread Christian monastic form, and its influence has spilled far beyond its own walls, for a number of other monastic orders (such as the Trappists, to which Thomas Merton belonged) amount to variations on the Benedictine theme. Benedictine houses abound in the Catholic Church, with hundreds of monasteries spread across every continent except Antarctica; Anglican, Lutheran, Orthodox, and ecumenical, nondenominational Benedictine monasteries also flourish around the globe. In addition, tens of thousands of laypeople, neither monks nor nuns, have struck spiritual bedrock by formally affiliating with a Benedictine monastery through a process known as oblation (described in greater detail in chapter 7).

It's not difficult to fathom the source of Benedict's enormous influence. His teaching shines with compassion and common sense. He treasures those things that never tarnish: learning, prayer, hospitality. As such, Benedictine monasteries have proven to be invaluable centers of peace and sanctity, particularly in eras of social turmoil. In Louis Malle's delightful 1980 film *My Dinner with Andre,* theater director Andre Gregory describes Benedictine monasteries during such epochs (for instance, between 600 and 900 in Europe) as "islands of safety where history can be remembered and the human being can continue to function, in order to maintain the species through a Dark Age"; the mission of these oases, he says, is "to preserve the light, life, the culture."[1] Gregory, who tends toward apocalyptic diagnoses, sees modern society as enshrouding itself in just such another Dark Age. While we may not share the grimness of his prophecy, there can be little doubt that the stress and strife of the contemporary world has done much to propel people toward monasteries and monastic retreat for spiritual renewal and rebirth.

In a sense, the monks and nuns of Petersham, Massachusetts, have hunkered down to a permanent retreat. All Benedictines make three promises upon donning the black habit. The first is *stability:* The monk or nun pledges to remain rooted (that is, to remain in retreat) for the rest of his or her life in the particular monastery where he or she lives. This can be a formidable discipline, especially in a nation like the United States, where John and Jane Doe switch residences, on average, once every eight years. At its most austere, in the case of cloistered communities—such as St. Mary's Monastery and St. Scholastica Priory—it means never leaving the enclosed grounds, except under exceptional circumstances. In former days, bars crisscrossed the windows, and those who chose the consecrated life addressed their infrequent visitors across an iron grille. These impressive security arrangements existed, it was said, not to lock in the monks and nuns, but to lock out the profane world. Within their enclosure, Benedictines find an exhilarating freedom, one that comes from dropping the demands of the ego in order to learn, as Abbot Denis Huerre, O.S.B., puts it, how to "breathe with God's own breath."[2]

The second Benedictine promise is that of *obedience,* especially to the head monk, or abbot (from the Aramaic *abba,* "father"). In asking for this pledge—so inflammatory to our ears today—Benedict didn't mean to suggest abject surrender to the abbot's every whim, but rather exactly the action that Abbot Huerre describes above: breaking the chains of self-love and substituting in their stead the unfettered love of God. Through obedience, the monk dies to self-will to be reborn in conformity to the will of God. As the earliest proto-monks of the Egyptian desert discovered, such obedience turns death to life, barrenness to abundance:

> They told this story of Abba John the Short. He went to an old man from the Thebaid, who was living in the desert of Scete. His abba once took a dead stick and planted it, and told him: "Pour a jug of water over its base every day until it bears fruit." Water was so far from their cell that he went away to fetch it every evening and did not return until dawn. At the end of three years the stick turned green, and bore fruit. The old man picked some of the fruit and took it to church, and said to the brothers, "Take and eat the fruit of obedience."[3]

The old man is each of us; the stick, our inner being; the planting, obedience; the water, spiritual practice; the fruit, renewal in love. But how can we know how or when or where to plant and water our stick, especially we who live outside of monasteries? How can we know the will of God? The best answer that I have heard to this crucial question, around which the entire monastic life revolves, came to me from Father Anselm Atkinson, religious superior at St. Mary's Monastery. "The will of God," he said, "is other people." We discern God's will—God's loving intentions for all creation—by turning from our own needs toward those of others (thus the renowned Benedictine emphasis on hospitality). Once again, we see that inner and outer work are one.

For the third promise, Benedict uses the Latin term *conversatio morum suorum,* an idiomatic expression whose meaning has been lost. The words translate literally as "the way of life of his behavior," an opaque expression at best. To circumvent the problem, sly monks for hundreds of years transcribed the phrase with *"conversio"* in place of *"conversatio."* This tiny erasure solves the problem, for the phrase then means "conversion of manners," or simply "conversion." In spite of its dubious provenance, this reading has become standard, a perfect example of the practicality and plasticity of the Benedictine way. As in the case of obedience, the meaning of conversion (or *conversio,* as Benedictines everywhere commonly refer to it) runs deeper than it may at first appear. Certainly, this promise has nothing to do with the modern notion of choosing one religion over another. Writing in the fifth century, Benedict took it for granted that his monks would be Christian; he would be startled, and I think delighted, by the multitude of non-Christians (especially, in the last few decades, Buddhist monks from Tibet and Japan) who have pored over his *Rule* with pleasure. Indeed for Benedict, *conversio* means something absolutely vital to real spiritual growth: the day-by-day, hour-by-hour, minute-by-minute, second-by-second work of inner transformation, the ever-renewed, continual turning from ourselves to God. Together, the three promises of stability, obedience, and *conversio* define the Benedictine way; they will play a major role on our retreat.

Appropriately enough, Benedict's teaching itself came about through a retreat, one of the most famous in Christian history. It took place during the first decades of the sixth century, as classical Roman civilization, over a thousand years old, crumbled under the assault of foreign invasions. Visigoths, Vandals, Huns, and other barbarian cultures hammered at the Eternal City's doors; blood flowed freely, disease rampaged, chaos reigned. Into this environment, Benedict was born (c. 480) in Nursia, a small town some forty miles south of Rome. While still a young man, he heard the call to holiness, and responded by withdrawing to a rocky grotto in the Anio

Valley north of Rome, overlooking a large artificial lake built by Nero. Here Benedict passed three years in total isolation, clad in animal skins, keeping silence, sustained by bread that a local peasant lowered to him on a rope.

Benedict's reputation for holiness soon spread beyond the confines of his hermitage. First a priest approached him, then shepherds, then members of a nearby monastery, who asked him to become their abbot. Benedict agreed, but the brethren soon rebelled at his severe regime (although, as we will see, it was remarkably moderate, even by modern standards). Not content with dismissing their abbot, they tried to poison him with tainted wine.

Understandably, Benedict returned to his grotto. Here, he redoubled his inner efforts, as St. Gregory the Great reports:

> Blessed Benedict . . . can be said to have lived "with himself" because at all times he kept such close watch over his life and actions. By searching continually into his own soul he always beheld himself in the presence of his Creator.[4]

If Benedict had remained in his cave, the history of Western civilization would have been vastly different. Happily, other monks soon petitioned the hermit, and before long Benedict had established twelve new monasteries, each consisting of a dozen monks and an abbot. Eventually, Benedict himself became abbot at Monte Cassino, built on the site of a temple of Apollo. The monastery stands to this day, albeit rebuilt from the ground up after Allied planes pounded it to rubble during World War II. There, according to Gregory, Benedict performed a number of miracles, such as expelling demons, instantly knitting broken bones, and foretelling the destruction of Rome. More enduringly, there he wrote his *Rule*.

We might fairly call the *Rule* Benedict's greatest miracle, for in this slim volume of no more than 18,000 Latin words divided into seventy-three terse chapters, Benedict set forever the course of Western monasticism. The *Rule* interweaves advice, admonishment, exhortation, and irony to great effect. It casts a warm eye on human frailties: "We read that monks should not drink wine at all, but since the monks of our day cannot be convinced of this, let us at least agree to drink moderately, and not to the point of excess" (*RB* 40). Yet it can be as strict as a one-room schoolmarm: "Permission to speak should seldom be granted even to mature disciples. . . . speaking and teaching are the master's task; the disciple is to be silent and listen" (*RB* 6). Above all, the *Rule* aims to teach monk or nun how to grow closer to God and to a blessed life; Abbot Huerre suggested a few years ago that Benedict's book might just as well be titled *The Art of Living*.

Every Benedictine monk or nun participates without fail in three daily occupations. These activities will become warp and woof of the daily fabric of our monastic retreat; they need to be examined in detail before we begin. In Latin, the trio has a lovely cadence that rolls lightly off the tongue: *oratio, labor, lectio divina*. In English, these translate into prayer, work, and sacred reading. Each occupation supports the others, and all are indispensable. Let us consider each in turn, and then weigh their cumulative effect.

ORATIO, OR PRAYER

At the Benedictine Monastic Center, the day begins at cockcrow, as monks and nuns hasten to the chapel for a forty-minute blend of chanted psalmody, scriptural reading, and silent prayer, known as Lauds. Six more Hours, as they are called (even though they may last but a few minutes), occur each day in keeping with the prescription in Psalm 119:164, "Seven times a day I praise you." (Some especially observant monasteries add an eighth Hour, known as the Night Office or Vigils, to conform to Psalm 119:62, "At midnight I rise to praise you.") The entire cycle is called the Divine Office or— the term preferred by Benedict—the *opus Dei* ("work of God"). Into this cryptic phrase, Benedict packs two essential meanings, for the work of God means both the work of prayer undertaken by every monk or nun, and God's work in the soul of everyone who prays. Of its importance, and the appropriate comportment of those who take part in it, Benedict writes that:

> We believe that the divine presence is everywhere. . . . But beyond the least doubt we should believe this to be especially true when we celebrate the divine office. . . . Let us consider, then, how we ought to behave in the presence of God and his angels, and let us stand to sing the psalms in such a way that our minds are in harmony with our voices. (*RB* 19)

Ideally, monks and nuns never "say" the Divine Office; they sing it, customarily in Gregorian chant. According to Benedict, the chant unfolds before all of creation, "in the presence of God and the angels," as well as that of human beings and even animals (I once saw a centipede march drunkenly down the nave as a group of four nuns, known as a *schola,* sang a lovely Latin *alleluia.* The centipede careened this way and that, in an ecstasy worthy of any saint, before coming to a dead stop in front of the altar, where, as far as I know, it said its centipedal prayers). Through the Divine Office, monks and nuns become a conduit between heaven and earth, singing prayers up to God and singing God's love down to us. They sing for all who cannot sing (including the little centipede), and they sing, tradition has it, in tandem with those whose song never ends, the cherubim, seraphim, and other angels whose voices soar beyond our normal range of hearing.

The seven Hours sanctify the daily round. Each phase of

the cycle—daybreak, early morning, mid-morning, high noon, afternoon, evening, sundown—finds its particular qualities reflected in the nature of its corresponding Hour, from the prismatic beauty of Lauds at daybreak to the intimacy of Compline as night closes in. Why seven Hours? Why not two or twenty-four? In part to satisfy the exclamation of the psalmist in the Hebrew Bible, "Seven times a day I praise you" (Psalms 119:164). In part, too, because seven notes (with the first repeated) constitute an octave. This measure appears throughout nature, in such fundamental structures as the musical scale, the periodic table of the elements, and the traditional model of the solar system. Benedict's arrangement thus adheres to cosmic law; the *opus Dei* reflects the basic form of God's creation.

The monastic community always assembles for the Hours; one very rarely sees a monk or nun chanting alone. Most houses spend a whopping amount of time in choir: At Petersham, the total averages about two-and-a-half hours each day, while at some other monasteries that figure doubles or even triples. At first glance, these numbers may scare us off, leading us to think that chant has no place in private retreat. Nothing could be further from the truth. Benedictine monks and nuns encourage everyone to chant the Divine Office whenever possible; it would be most unmonastic to claim such a glorious activity as one's private preserve. I have found, from my own experience, that the Office can be tailored to suit a personal retreat, whether conducted alone or with others, without doing violence to its basic nature.

For our three-day retreat, I propose that we restrict ourselves to the three most important Hours: Lauds, Vespers, and Compline. We will use for our texts the same selection of psalms, canticles, and biblical passages sung in Benedictine monasteries throughout the world (abbreviated here and there to accommodate our particular needs). I propose, in addition, that we chant the Hours at the same times each day as do the monks and nuns inhabiting our local time zone. Through this close adherence to universal monastic practice, we will enjoy one of the principal blessings conferred by the Divine Office: the knowledge that we join our voices to those of 10,000 others, a chain of prayer running around the globe, linked tightly to the great chain of prayer extending back through time to Moses, and before.

In addition to praying the Divine Office, each Benedictine monk or nun devotes a portion of his or her day to private prayer. Such prayer ranges from contemplation to vocal petitions to specific techniques such as the Jesus Prayer. On our retreat, we will become acquainted with all of these methods; specific information is given in later chapters. We will find, beneath their varied form, that all private prayers share a paradoxical double action. First, they initiate a new inner order, described by St. Paul as the "new self" awakened to God; second, they open us to God, who in turn reorders us into the new self. Asking which of these events comes first is a chicken-and-egg conundrum: Each supports the other; anyone who prays will soon know the taste of both.

LABOR, OR WORK

Monks and nuns engage in all sorts of work. They boil jam, breed dogs, sew vestments, keep bees, "write" icons (as the painting of these strange, flat images is properly called), all this in addition to the jobs that crop up whenever any group of people gather, such as cooking, sweeping, nursing, and the like; and all this on top of the many hours spent in the *opus Dei* and private prayer. As anyone who has visited a monastery can testify, sometimes (not too often!) the bustle smacks more of the corporate office than the Divine Office. Most of this activity brings in money to keep the ship afloat, each monastery being responsible for its own upkeep. Some enterprises—weaving, silk-screening, printing, and the like—result in objects of striking beauty that, monastics believe, reflect the beauty of God. For this reason, among others, craft flourishes at most Benedictine houses.

At the same time, manual labor regulates the daily life of each monk and nun as surely as does the Divine Office (we hear echoes here of the lovely Shaker apothegm "hands to work, hearts to God"). Working with one's hands also serves as a splendid opportunity for self-study, and thus a means of putting into practice lessons absorbed beneath reading lamps in the monastic library. While bumbling through our work, we may catch a glimpse of ourselves as we really are, not as we imagine ourselves to be. My fantasies of being a master potter, for example, scooted closer to reality after just a few hours on the wheel, watching my precious bowls (so perfect in my mind's eye) revert to blobs and globs. I keep one of these bowls on my desk even now, a clay mirror that never lies. Such self-knowledge forms the necessary backdrop for transformation; for how can we enter "the kingdom of God within" without a road map of our inner terrain? Making such a sketch of our follies—and, to be sure, our occasional successes—is a principal reward of manual labor. We will make much use of it on our three-day retreat, trying out a number of different activities, sustaining them as long as they prove fruitful, and then turning to something new.

LECTIO DIVINA, OR SACRED READING

During my years as a professional book reviewer, often I would find my desk groaning under the weight of the latest publishing crop, books piled high in mounds, pinnacles, and teetering towers, books of every species under the sun, crime thrillers and logic studies, fishing manuals and poetry collections, ancient myths and New Age channelings, cookbooks with no kitchen in sight, coffee-table books that I would shield as best I could from the contents of my leaking coffee cup. My job obliged me to review almost all these volumes; sometimes I read so many words in a single day that my head whirled, my stomach churned, and when I closed my eyes I could see nothing but countless armies of letters marching forever across an endless page. I fell asleep more than once to the frightful fancy that my blanket and mattress had become a book jacket, and I was the dreaded reading material in between. But how would I read myself? This metaphysical puzzle would trap me for hours in that queasy half-awake, half-asleep land where tiny mental torments swell to elephantine size (at last, I am happy to report, I learned to relax into sleep simply by asking God, the master reviewer, to read *me* cover to cover).

In self-defense, I soon became adept at the secret skill of every book reviewer, a talent that all possess but none whisper abroad. I learned to skim. Skimming is not skipping, nor is it skimping; skimming is sliding down the page lickety-split, gobbling up everything, but spitting most of it out as soon as its flavor becomes clear, while the mind absorbs only those passages that, through some sixth sense peculiar to heavy readers, contain the real meat and potatoes. Skimming works—but not always. As I discovered, three kinds of reading matter resist all skimming. The first two are novels and poems, where every word, every image, every sound counts. The third is scripture. Here, too, everything matters. But in addition a new factor comes into play: According to every religious tradition in the world, in the inviolable words of scripture we can discover truth itself.

While reading scripture, then—and I did have to read it occasionally, for I specialized in books on religion—I learned to listen with the utmost attention, to ruminate on each word, sentence, paragraph, insofar as I was capable of such a trying feat. "Ruminate" seems to be the only word that fits, for just as a cow chews its cud, we need to chew the words of scripture, to extract all the meaning, veiled or revealed. No easy task! For scripture (and this goes for all sacred texts, for Koran and Pali Canon as well as Holy Bible) consists of overlapping layers of content, style, and intention, which must be peeled and savored one by one. Scripture, I discovered, resembles more a complicated piece of high cuisine than a candy that melts compliantly in the mouth.

Although I didn't know it at the time, in mulling over scripture in my weak and amateurish way, I was on the road to discovering the third daily task of monks and nuns, which Benedict called *lectio divina,* or sacred reading. A monk or nun reads slowly, reflectively, meditating on each passage. Often the words become glued to the mind, enter into permanent memory, and surface when needed in times of prayer. For the first millennium or so of Christian monasticism, monks and nuns read aloud, with such vigor that some medieval texts describe reading as an athletic activity. Like all good exercise, sacred reading brings ample rewards. As the monk reads, it is said, the scripture enters his heart; and God, who dwells in the scripture, slips in as well.

Traditional monastic practice restricts *lectio divina* to scripture or patristic works. However, I believe that we can remain faithful to the monastic tradition during our retreat while expanding our selection of texts to include any dignified reading that brings us closer to God. Certainly, the most secure choice remains the Bible. But let us embrace whatever will help. Who can say what word, what text, what author will escort someone into the holy of holies? In *Pilgrim at Tinker Creek,* Annie Dillard mentions a plethora of odd titles—my favorite is *The Gentle Art of Tramping,* described as "antique and elegant"—that she devoured on retreat. The guidelines are simple: Read, don't glance; pore over the text with open eyes and a steady heart, as if your life depended on it, as indeed it does. In the next chapter, the choice of books appropriate for retreat is discussed in detail.

What then of the cumulative effect of *oratio, labor,* and *lectio divina?* Where does all this point us? Let us return for a moment to *oratio,* prayer: We sing the Divine Office with larynx and lungs, with head, heart, and soul; swept up by the chant, we fly to God, finding in our ascent a unity of being that too often eludes us. Particulars aside, this description applies equally well to all other monastic activities, to private prayer, manual labor, and sacred reading. In one and all, we look to be whole; we look for God, in whom we find our wholeness. We look for balance, the balance that we find only when resting in the hands of God. I believe that through a monastic retreat based on Benedictine principles and practices, we will find something of what we seek. The Benedictine way teaches us, as Denis Huerre so memorably puts it, how "to live so that we are glad to be alive."[5] It seems to me that in these words we have a suitable goal for our retreat, and for our life as well.

Part Two

RETREAT

And after he had
dismissed the crowds,
he went up the mountain
by himself to pray.

—Matthew 14:23

Chapter Three

PREPARATIONS

One of my favorite moun-
tain-climbing stories in-
volves the eccentric ex-
plorer Maurice Wilson. In the 1930s, this thirty-eight-year-old
Englishman hatched the harebrained scheme of tackling Mt.
Everest alone. There was something glorious in Wilson's
madcap dream, for he pinned his hopes on faith in God,
whom he believed would guide him safely to the summit, and
on the extraordinary resilience of the human body, which he
thought could withstand the brutal deprivation of oxygen,
warmth, and food that the assault on Everest entailed. Wilson
was last seen trudging up the mountain's north face at 21,000
feet, carrying nothing but three loaves of bread, two cans of
porridge, a British flag, and a camera. He never came back
down, and his body was never recovered. Fifty years later, it's
impossible to think of Wilson's exploit without admiring his
pluck—how grand those old, solitary adventurers were—and
without shaking our heads at his foolhardiness. In his frozen
fate lies an important lesson for our retreat: Faith can carry
you very far, but planning counts as well.

Although the Bible describes many retreats, it offers few clues about proper preparation. Happily, though, we aren't abandoned to our own devices, for millions of Christians have trekked before us into the spiritual hinterlands, and many of them have bequeathed us helpful hints and cautions. One suggestion crops up so frequently that it might be called the Golden Rule of Retreat: *Less is more.* The fewer encumbrances we lug along, the more time and space we make available for God. The classic cartoon of a Wall Street tycoon punching away at his calculator while sunbathing on a Caribbean beach conveys a message applicable to religious retreat as well: At all costs, we must leave the world and its demands behind. We have other work to do. For the brief period of our retreat, the outside world does not exist. Shopping lists, bits of office business, "essential" phone calls, all add up to nothing but clutter. This excess baggage often sneaks in wearing the friendly mask of "spiritual" paraphernalia. Beware of too many sacred books, too many meditations, too many ambitions. All these have their place, but on retreat they can be akin to the weights and chains that Jacob Marley's ghost dragged around as symbols of his avarice.

Stripping down to essentials is only the first step. We need to address a number of other specific issues to ensure that our retreat bears abundant fruit.

Choosing a Time and Place

The trophy for the strangest retreat site in history goes to St. Simeon Stylites (390–459), who endured twenty-three years atop a sixty-seven-foot-high pillar in the Egyptian desert. On this remarkable perch, only six feet wide, Simeon ate, slept, and prayed. He undertook this almost inconceivable feat of athletic asceticism in order to tame both inner and outer demons. No doubt great suffering was involved, but we may safely assume that Simeon had a head for heights and considerable tolerance for cramped living quarters. I don't encourage any of us to follow his example, although a faint echo of Simeon's experience can be heard in the ecstasies of Maurice Wilson and other mountaineers atop lofty peaks, as well as the mystical trance that swept over astronaut Edward White during his pioneering 1965 space walk (a species of retreat that few of us may have the chance to enjoy), prompting him to refuse at first to return to the *Gemini IV* capsule.

Most of us, I suspect, will prefer a more mundane site for our retreat. Nonetheless, we must select the location with special care. It will become for us sacred territory, the hallowed ground before the burning bush, the arena of encounter with God. Moses, John the Baptist, Jesus, and a host of others chose the wilderness because of its affinity for spiritual renewal, as a land where angels and devils tromped, where heaven bent down to earth. Figuratively, at least, we must search out our own wilderness for our retreat.

No doubt, many of us find the idea of scooting off to desert or mountain no more appealing than a voyage to the lunar wastes. Practical reasons will dictate, in most cases, that our retreat take place at home. It's best to arrange affairs so that we have the location to ourselves; wait until the kids have been packed off to summer camp, or that loud roommate has taken her long-anticipated vacation to the South Pacific. A home retreat offers obvious advantages: All necessities lie close at hand, no hidden expenses crop up (such as the cost of renting a campsite), and—of no small importance—security is assured. Temporary shelter, such as a woodland tent, lean-to, or cabin, affords a second possibility. Here we can count on remoteness, but safety becomes a concern. Set up camp in a secure spot, so that intruders (human or animal) won't become a distraction, or worse. As a third alternative, contact one of the many private retreat centers strewn across the United States and Europe; these organizations offer an assortment of cabins, group houses, and other accommodations in forest, field, or mountain. Finally, one may take refuge in a Benedictine monastery (nearly 100 dot the continental United States alone). Most monastic communities offer private rooms in exchange for a small donation, invariably waived for those who can't afford to pay. As I indicated in chapter 2, the advantages of monastery-based retreats abound, including secluded spots for private prayer, the presence of senior monks or nuns who might be available for guidance, the chance to participate in the community's liturgical life (including the Divine Office), and above all, the holy atmosphere that pervades these "school[s] for the Lord's service," as Benedict describes them (*RB*, prol.).

Whether house, hill, or monastic haven, our place of retreat needs to be outfitted ahead of time. We should stock up on staples (food, toilet paper, batteries, and so on), to avoid unnecessary excursions to the local market. Nothing is more jarring, in the midst of a retreat, than suddenly to find oneself eyeball-to-eyeball with the garish headlines of tabloid newspapers on the checkout line. All pressing business should be settled ahead of time or postponed until after the retreat has ended; we must be able to immerse ourselves fully in the task at hand. Once, on a large group retreat that lasted seven days, I volunteered to be the gofer, dashing out at all hours to fetch everything from frozen strawberries for the cook to a new ladder for the building team. At week's end, our house shone with new white walls, and the fruit pie sat benevolently in our stomachs, but the retreat had been for me largely a shambles, a disorienting succession of comings and goings, in which the zeal for material success had drowned out the needs of the heart.

Choosing the Right Equipment

No spiritual work takes place in a vacuum. Jesus made use of material supports: spit and mud to cure blindness; Torah for prayer; fish, wine, and bread as signs of God's bounty. We too require material aids for our spiritual work. Among the most important are sitting tools, books, and prayer beads.

Sitting Tools

We will spend much of our time in sitting: not lounging, lazing, cuddling, curling, snoozing, or slouching, but *sitting,* back straight, mind alert, heart awake in prayer. For prolonged contemplation, the spine should be as erect as possible, both to support attention and to allow the unimpeded flow of subtle energies throughout the body. Christian monks and nuns, particularly in the Greek and Russian Orthodox Churches, have made a thorough study of the psychophysical aspects of meditation and prayer. From their massive research, we need only extract the observation that any tension, muscular or nervous, can be fatal to our efforts. We can do nothing without a relaxed body. This insistence on somatic states may surprise some people, but every aspect of the monastic way depends on the body, for all depend ultimately on the traditional teaching of the Incarnation. "God became what we are that we might become what God is," as St. Irenaeus put it. In the body we meet God; in the body God met us, 2,000 years ago in Palestine; and in the body God meets us still.

For sitting in prayer, many people prefer a hard, straight-backed chair. However, a number of other appliances have been devised to help us sit for long periods; all bear consideration. The *seiza* bench, a low wooden affair consisting of a plank with two legs, offers exceptional stability and comfort. One sits on the plank and tucks one's feet underneath. However, an average-sized *seiza* bench doesn't suit large people (such as myself), who with knees scrunched together and leg muscles pulled taut may feel like Gulliver in a Lilliputian meditation hall. But the *seiza* bench can be supremely supportive for smaller folk, as the gentle slant of the plank does much to keep the spine erect. Another possibility, unknown outside of *zendos* thirty years ago but seen everywhere these days, is a *zafu* (meditation cushion), either by itself or mounted for added height on a series of flat pillows. One may straddle the cushion, knees apart, with the pillow tucked into one's crotch (my preferred position), or if one has the knack for bending like a pretzel, one can sit in a half-lotus or lotus position. The important thing is comfort, so that we can remain still for a long stretch—at least thirty minutes—without pain or fidgeting.

Books

Fritz Peters, who wrote several books about his childhood with the Russian spiritual teacher George Gurdjieff, once remarked that Gurdjieff's establishment at Fontainbleau, France, had the most remarkable library he had ever seen: It contained nary a single book. Although we needn't follow Gurdjieff's example, the message behind this extraordinary collection (or lack thereof) compels our attention: Most books offer little except distraction and don't belong on retreat. Books have voices, as surely as do people: When we ask what books to bring, in effect we ask which voices will break the silence of our weekend. One of the most famous stories in the Bible recounts the retreat of Elijah in a cave on Mt. Horeb:

> And behold, the Lord passed by, and a great and strong wind rent the mountains, and broke in pieces the rocks before the Lord, but the Lord was not in the wind; and after the wind an earthquake, but the Lord was not in the earthquake; and after the earthquake a fire, but the Lord was not in the fire; and after the fire a still small voice. *(1 Kings 19:11–12, RSV)*

We too must let whirlwinds, earthquakes, and conflagrations pass by, seeking instead the "still small voice" of God: a voice so gentle, so muted, that the clamor of ordinary life easily drowns it out. In order to hear this voice, we must silence the world: thus the prohibition on materials that inflame our emotions or senses, or that draw us back into our ordinary worries and obsessions. This includes not only reading related to our jobs, but also books that trade in sensationalism or gossip. Beach-chair bestsellers should be avoided. Journalism will also contaminate the special atmosphere we are trying to foster; I recommend that all newspapers and magazines that cater to ephemeral interests (*Time, Life, The New Yorker,* and so on) be left behind or placed out of sight.

What reading will help us in our search for God? Possibilities include:

The Holy Bible: Both Christianity and Judaism esteem the Bible as the inspired word of God. In the course of reciting the Divine Office, we will become familiar with many scriptural psalms and canticles. Please don't limit your experience to these brief tastes, however. I urge you to open the Bible anywhere and read attentively; you will not fail to be rewarded.

Rule *of St. Benedict:* I advise you to tote along the *Rule,* which you can pick up for a few dollars at many bookstores. Opening it at random can pay rich dividends, or you may wish to read the entire book during the retreat. In particular, I recommend close study of chapters 4 through 7, in which Benedict lays the foundations of monastic practice through his discussions of obedience, silence, humility, and what he calls "tools for good works"—seventy-one counsels beginning with the scriptural injunction to "love the Lord God with your whole heart, your whole soul and all your strength," and concluding with "never lose hope in God's mercy" (*RB* 4).

Anthologies of prayer and poetry: The Book of Common Prayer and similar prayer books offer many possibilities for *lectio divina*. Religious poetry also sits well on retreat. I favor the seventeenth-century metaphysical poets (John Donne, George Herbert, Richard Crawshaw), but you will have your own favorites.

Monastic writings: It goes without saying that books by monks and nuns will help us to savor the full flavor of Christian monasticism. Recommended texts include:

> ➤ St. Athanasius, *Life of Antony.* The classic life of the prototypical monk.

> ➤ John Chapman, *Selected Letters.* Letters on contemplative prayer by the late abbot of Downside Abbey, England.

> ➤ Felicitas Corrigan, *A Benedictine Tapestry.* Collected essays on monasticism by a nun of Stanbrook Abbey, England.

> ➤ St. Gregory the Great, *Life of St. Benedict.* The traditional biography.

> ➤ Thomas Keating, M. Basil Pennington, Thomas E. Clarke, *Finding Grace at the Center.* A superb collection of writings on contemplative prayer.

> ➤ Thomas Merton, *The Contemplative Life.* The rudiments of monastic spirituality, by the well-known Cistercian monk.

Prayer Beads

In Istanbul's Grand Bazaar, that vast underground labyrinth of teahouses, kebab stands, and mile upon mile of ramshackle shops smelling of incense and yogurt, the grizzled old man sidled up to me, eyes aglitter. "You like my rugs," he said in thickly accented English, "the most beautiful rugs in the world." He was right; I had been furtively admiring a cream-and-rose prayer rug that had won my heart. Although I tried to be surreptitious—friends had warned me about the legendary rapaciousness of the bazaar hawkers—the old man zeroed in on the carpet I coveted.

"Perfect weave," he said. "Worth much, very much." He then named an impossibly high price. I countered with a bargain-basement figure. We bickered back and forth, while sipping from copper cups of steaming sweet tea, a ubiquitous accompaniment to all wheeling and dealing in Turkey. Our palaver went nowhere, and finally the salesman threw up his hands and exclaimed, "No sale, my friend," and handed me his business card for future use. I slipped it into my jacket.

In the process, my watchband snagged on something inside my pocket. I tugged, and out fell a Christian prayer rope—a thick black circlet of cord braided into fifty knots, with a small cloth cross depending from it. I had bought the rope a few months earlier, in order to practice the Jesus Prayer (see chapter 5 for a description of this prayer). The salesman swooped down and snatched it up. "Ah, prayers!" he barked. "You do prayers!" He then pulled from his own pocket a nearly identical rope, and waggled it before my eyes. The only obvious difference was that the cross was replaced by a thick tuft of dangling threads. "I do prayers too," he said, beaming at me like a long-lost brother. He then gave me a deep look and said, "Now we can do business." Twenty minutes later, I walked out of the bazaar with my prayer rug bundled under my arm.

Thanks to this gruff Turkish shopkeeper, I had stumbled on the noblest of secret societies: the universal union of prayer-rope users. We tend to define religions by their differences, epitomized in their distinguishing signs: Cross, Koran, bodhi tree. But, as I have learned, the prayer rope binds together almost every faith on earth. In Tibet, Egypt, Ireland, Chile—wherever people pray (and where don't people pray?)—the prayer rope is found. It serves, above all, as a mnemonic aid, to keep one's place in a complex sequence of worship. It also reminds one of the commitment to the inner life. The cord's rough texture, its comforting thickness when nestled in a pocket, the clack of the beads (most prayer ropes have beads of plastic, glass, bone, or seashell in place of knots; my wife owns a small one, known as a chaplet, beaded with compressed rose petals) all summon us to prayer. Finally, it symbolizes the great rope of prayer that binds us to all who pray and all who have prayed, in every faith and every land.

Christian prayer ropes come in two forms: as a rosary (with beads) or as a knotted cord. By and large, Western Christianity favors rosary beads, while Eastern forms promote the cord (known by the generic term of "prayer rope"). However, these boundaries are fluid. On the second day of our retreat, we will try our hand at the Jesus Prayer; although most people associate this technique with the prayer rope, rosary beads work just as well and will be much easier to obtain (they can be purchased in most religious bookstores). I recommend picking up a set of rosary beads or a prayer rope before beginning the retreat; it will ground and elevate your experience in prayer.

Miscellaneous Tools

Because of its doctrines of creation and incarnation, Christianity has always placed great importance on physical signs of God's presence. This explains, for example, the significance of miracle stories—changing water into wine, restoring sight to the blind, and so on—throughout the New Testament and, indeed, throughout the history of the Church. It also underlies the traditional use of material objects to help one commune with God. In addition to rosary and prayer rope, such items include icons, incense, flowers, candles, and the like. I urge you to incorporate into your monastic retreat whatever materials will enhance your time of prayer. Nothing focuses the mind better than erecting a prayer niche with an icon in the center, perhaps accompanied by a sprig of winterberry or a few roses, with a chair or sitting cushion facing the sacred image. The majority of icons, painted according to an ancient, quasi-esoteric methodology, depict either Christ in his cosmic aspect (Christ Pantocrator), or Virgin and Child. These images, as well as ancillary items such as incense, can be readily obtained at most religious book shops.

KEEPING A JOURNAL

Some years ago, while I was away at college, my parents moved from Long Island to a suburb of Philadelphia. Many precious childhood possessions vanished during this upheaval, including my violin and telescope, magic carpets into the enchanted realms of art and science. But nothing pained me so much as the loss of my journals. I had begun them at the age of thirteen and had inscribed in them all the triumphs and terrors of adolescence, recording events both exterior (friends made, books read, inventions built) and interior (puppy romances, pet peeves). Even now, decades later, I remember a few of the most important notations, and that affords some consolation. Yet the loss remains irreparable, and it drilled a lesson home. By their absence, I learned how much I prize such records of my life. To this day I keep a journal; needless to say, I safeguard it zealously.

Each of us should maintain a journal while on retreat. Nearly everyone who tries his or her hand at it reaps rewards;

one needn't be a Samuel Pepys to enjoy the form. Don't be shy: Write in your journal every day, even if you believe that you have nothing to say. Never let the page remain blank for long; nothing is more intimidating, even for professional writers, than a broad sheet of unmarked white. Turn it black, fast. If necessary, pour onto the paper whatever comes into your head, regardless of value. Soon, your critical faculties will sharpen, and you will learn to edit as you write.

Try to transcribe your feelings from heart to page. If this embarrasses you, simply describe what you see, hear, smell, taste, touch. Your way of doing this—what you choose to include or omit, what you emphasize, what words you pick to frame your observations—will also reveal your feelings. Write down dreams, warnings, speculations, memories, notions, imprecations, idylls, intimations of paradise. Write about the world you have left and the world you wish to reenter. Write about friends, foes, family, about anything and everything. Write only for yourself, without fear or inhibition. "But I already know what I think," you protest. "Why write it down?" In the answer to this question lies the great secret behind all composition. Truth be told, none of us knows what we think. We believe that we do—but we know it inchoate, without structure, sequence, or coloration. Writing itself gives birth to thought, to vision, to unsuspected and vital landscapes. Keeping a journal will deepen your retreat beyond imagining.

Choosing a Saint

I will never forget my first visit to the island of Malta, that limestone chip of dusky gold in the blue-green Mediterranean from which my mother's family hails. One day my great-aunt Nena, a jolly white-haired woman well into her eighties, escorted my wife, my mother, and me to the church of Madonna

Tal-Herba (Maltese for "Madonna of the Ruins") in Birkikara, a town just a few miles from the capital of Valetta. Here, in a shadowy chapel basement, hung score upon score of votive offerings: canes, walkers, artificial limbs, and crude illustrations in charcoal or oil (some of them executed by my maternal grandfather) of ship sinkings, car crashes, volcanic eruptions, and other spectacular disasters. Each of these odd donations, my great aunt told us, commemorates a miracle. This battered crutch belonged to a young girl healed of lameness; this painting depicts a sailor snatched from a shark's chomping jaws. Invariably, the lucky survivors ascribe their escape to Madonna Tal-Herba or to their patron saint. Few care to disagree. Who can argue with men and women who have come within a hairsbreadth of death and thus have earned the right to speak their minds? In this dimly lit cellar, I saw demonstrated in all its grit and grandeur the ancient Christian practice of devotion to the saints.

From earliest times, Christians have turned to their holy predecessors for help. Some of us may find it strange to pray to the dead, even the saintly dead. Yet the custom crops up in nearly every religion. The saints link earth and heaven, life and afterlife. By virtue of their exemplary lives, it is said, they now sit with God. One prays to a saint to intercede with God, fountain of all goodness. The saint becomes a beloved friend, to whom one turns for advice, succor, and companionship. This sense of solidarity between the living and the dead, between the saints and the rest of us, has been put most beautifully by a saint herself, Thérèse of Lisieux, who just before her death from tuberculosis in 1896 at the age of twenty-four wrote, "I want to spend my heaven doing good on earth."

I realize that a few of us may wonder at the idea of saintly intercession, based as it is on anecdotal evidence that stubbornly resists scientific analysis. Some will straddle the fence:

"A lovely idea," we say, *"if only it were true."* Others will go a bit further, confessing, "I believe that an invisible world exists, the realm of angels, saints, and God. But I don't understand its nature or its relation to our own." To this last admission, the only honest response is, "Who does?" To the skeptical and the hesitant, I ask that you adopt—only as an experiment, for the three days of our retreat—the same state of mind that Coleridge considered essential for poets, the "willing suspension of disbelief." It may be that holding doubts at bay will open the door to unexpected vistas, as it led Schliemann to Troy. I urge you to pray to a saint throughout the retreat. Pray to her as a friend, an intimate, as someone who knows your sufferings, your hopes. Pray that she watch over you, protect you, and give you strength; pray that she light your way to God.

Which saint, you may ask, will be right for me? A fair question, for, to paraphrase what Tolstoy said about families in the first sentence of *Anna Karenina,* "Every saint is dissimilar in his or her own way." Every saint is radically himself or herself. We call them saints for just this reason: not because they have erased their individual identities by drinking a bland potion called "sanctity," but because in their very surrender of self they have realized themselves to the full. One can find no better expression of this than the unforgettable saying attributed to Rabbi Zusya: "When I die, God will not ask me, 'Why were you not Moses?' Surely He will ask me, 'Why were you not Zusya?'"

The names of eight saints appear on the list below. To some extent, the selection is arbitrary. I might just as easily have listed eight—or eight thousand—others, for all saints deserve study and prayer. Those chosen cover the spectrum of types: young and old, educated and illiterate, ancient and modern.

At first, you may pray to your saint while knowing little about her, perhaps no more than is contained in the thumbnail sketches below. No matter; there will be ample time to research her life and miracles after the retreat ends (or before it begins, if you plan ahead). For now, simply form an impression of your saint based on the notes below and on your own intuition. This will suffice; remember, she is there to help you.

One more bit of advice: Please don't feel bound to the names on this list, or even to the formal catalog of canonized saints. Perhaps the saintliest person in your life is your deceased grandmother; then pray to her.

The Blessed Virgin Mary: The highest and most beloved of the saints, traditionally acclaimed as *Theotokos,* Mother of God.

St. Joseph: The Husband of the Blessed Virgin Mary. A simple carpenter revered for his unique role as a protector of the Holy Family. Patron saint of workers and travelers; venerated as a devoted family man.

St. Benedict: The founder of Western monasticism. See chapter 2 for more information.

St. Scholastica: The twin sister of St. Benedict. A cloistered nun, best known for a single, perhaps legendary, event. During one of her rare visits with Benedict, Scholastica was dismayed when her brother rose abruptly to return to his monastery. She prayed for a storm to detain him. God instantly obliged, as lightning flashed and rain fell in torrents. In Benedictine tradition, Scholastica's prayer exemplifies the primacy of love over all ascetic considerations.

St. Mary Magdalene: A close follower of Jesus and the first to see him after his resurrection, a sign of special honor. The prototype of the sinner who becomes a saint; patron of all who mend their ways.

St. Francis of Assisi: "Il povorello" (the little poor man), loved for his kindness, humility, and sacrifice. Patron saint of ecology.

St. Maximilian Kolbe: A contemporary saint, martyred by the Nazis. Interred at Auschwitz, Kolbe volunteered to take the place of another man condemned to death, and was executed with an injection of carbolic acid. The person whose life he saved was present at Kolbe's canonization ceremony in 1982.

St. Thérèse of Lisieux: The most celebrated modern saint, author of the extraordinary autobiography *The Story of a Soul.* A paragon of humility and simplicity, founder of the "little way." For more on St. Thérèse, see chapters 4 and 6.

SETTING AN AIM

Every so often I teach a college class in nature writing, a literary genre that demands, among other things, a knack for observing nature in the raw. A few weeks into the course, one issue arises without fail: how to get ready for our field trips. All agree on the need for physical groundwork: gathering insect repellent, notebooks, pencils, sunscreen, first-aid kit, water bottles, and the like. Debate rages, however, over what other preliminaries may be required; in particular, whether we should read background material to get a sense of what to expect before plunging into the wilderness. Some students say no, insisting that this will prejudice us against new experience. We will see only what we expect to see, and the freshly minted glories of nature will escape our eyes. Others say yes: We must supply our minds as well as our rucksacks, they argue, or we will lack compasses both mental and material. To help settle the argument, I have the students read the following passage from Thoreau's essay on "Seeing":

> Nature does not cast pearls before swine. There is just as much beauty visible to us in the landscape as we are prepared to appreciate,—not a grain more. . . . The scarlet oak must, in a sense, be in your eye when you go forth. We cannot see anything until we are possessed with the idea of it. . . . I find that first the idea, or image, of a plant occupies my thoughts, though it may at first seem very foreign to this locality, and for some weeks or months I go thinking of it and expecting it unconsciously, and at length I surely see it, and it is henceforth an actual neighbor of mine. This is the history of my finding a score or more of rare plants which I could name.

Thus speaks the master literary woodsman: Without preparation, we will see nothing. To underscore this idea, I remind my students of the eating habits of the common frog. The frog cannot see a stationary insect; the idea of a nonmoving food supply lies beyond the scope of its amphibian brain. If someday we met an intelligent frog and explained to it that insects continue to exist while standing still, this knowledge might open up a vast new empire, a worldwide bug-restaurant of sorts, for that lucky frog. So it is with us as well. When someone blind from birth acquires sight, at first he or she sees the world as smears and blurs and blobs of color. Time must pass before that trembling brown rope topped with green settles down and becomes a maple tree, before that soft white ball six feet off the ground becomes a lover's face. We need to be ready to meet our experience.

In exactly the same way, we should clarify our aims before we go on retreat. Only by having a goal toward which we strive will our daily struggles acquire meaning, savor, substantial value. What wishes do we hold dear for this time apart? We might want to discover new resources to help us in our everyday lives. But what does this mean, exactly? Do we hope to find a measure of peace with ourselves and others, to root out a bad habit, to awaken to God's presence, to surrender to God's love? Our goal may be simply to meet God for the first time. No small aim, that. All such inspirations are legitimate; all spur us on.

After pondering this question for a sufficient length of time (you must decide for yourself how long that is), write down your aim for the retreat in your journal.

THE PATTERN OF THE RETREAT

Snowflakes have patterns, as do symphonies and stories. All beautiful things have harmonic structure, and so should our retreat. At the same time, we must remain supple enough to accommodate whatever unexpected adventures and lessons each day brings. The best course, once again, is moderation. Luckily for us, just such a pattern—firm in outline, but plastic in detail—lies right at hand. We find it in the symbolic meaning of Friday, Saturday, and Sunday, the three days of our retreat. (I assume that most of us plan to hold our retreat on a weekend, but any three successive days will fit the design.)

These three days hearken back to the three most sacred days in Christian history: Good Friday, Holy Saturday, and Easter Sunday, which witnessed the death and resurrection of Christ. We can do no better than to base our retreat on this sacred model, for whatever our particular aims, we all share the universal wish to die to dessicated ways, dead habits, dead-end dreams, and to rise to a new life of vitality and hope. No one expresses this wish more eloquently than St. Paul:

> You have stripped off the old self with its practices and have clothed yourselves with the new self, which is being renewed in knowledge according to the image of its creator. . . . Clothe

yourselves with compassion, kindness, humility, meekness, and patience. Bear with one another and, if anyone has a complaint against another, forgive each other; just as the Lord has forgiven you, so you also must forgive. Above all, clothe yourselves with love, which binds everything together in perfect harmony.

(Colossians 3:9–10, 12–14)

In traditional Christian symbolism, Friday is the day of death, of letting go. On Friday we surrender to God's call of love and to our own desire for transformation. Saturday begins the process of renewal, a day of struggles matched by satisfactions. Sunday is the day of resurrection or rebirth, on which we rejoice in our newfound life. This three-part template, sanctified by Christ's example, has inspired millions of men and women through twenty centuries. I believe that we make a wise choice by adopting it for our retreat.

Happily, the monastic practices we will incorporate into our retreat fit neatly into this tripartite pattern. Monks and nuns participate in three fundamental modes of prayer: thanksgiving, petition, and adoration. In the first, we thank God for blessing us; in the second, we ask God for assistance; in the third, we acknowledge, praise, and venerate God as the ultimate mystery, source of all being, the "I AM THAT I AM" of Exodus. All three types of prayer will play a role in our retreat; we will emphasize one each day (while not neglecting the other two). The same pattern applies to the three monastic promises of stability, obedience, and *conversio*. We will emphasize stability on Friday, obedience on Saturday, and *conversio* on Sunday, while drawing sustenance from all each day.

To lend backbone to our retreat, every day we will try our hand at the Divine Office, manual labor, and *lectio divina*. Together, these constitute the axis of our retreat, around which all other activities revolve. We should therefore make every effort to join in each of these activities as regularly and completely as possible. At the same time, let us bear in mind that we have withdrawn from ordinary life in search of prayer and perspective, not imprisonment. Each of us must decide for himself or herself when discipline becomes hidebound and laxness becomes sloppiness. Some people thrive on a flexible structure, and find that a Spartan regime stifles creativity. Too many "spiritual exercises" can be another way of stuffing the day with business in order to avoid the real work of inner renewal. Other people require a firm framework in which to grow, like the wooden latticework that supports the climbing rose. There is nothing more discouraging on retreat than to find oneself stuck in a corner with nothing to do. To avoid this cul-de-sac, our retreat program distributes a number of varied activities throughout the day. None of them will suit everyone. All, of course, are optional. Please remember: This retreat belongs to you.

The diagram opposite shows the overall pattern of our retreat.

THE NIGHT BEFORE

Several years ago, when my interest in Christian monasticism had just begun to bloom, I scheduled a weekend retreat at St. Joseph's Abbey, a Cistercian monastery for men outside the small town of Spencer, Massachusetts. The abbey's guest list fills up quickly, and I made my reservations nine months in advance. As the day of the retreat crept near, I began to fidget. This would be my first overnight stay in a monastery, and I had no idea what to expect. What if I didn't fit in? What if the monks turned out to be creepy? What if my wife needed me at home? The worrier within me held center court.

By the time the great day arrived, I was a nervous wreck. Driving up to the monastery gates, my stomach flip-flopped and a jackhammer pounded in my skull. I grabbed my bags,

PATTERN OF THE RETREAT

Day One

Theme:	Detachment, or death
Prayer:	Thanksgiving
Prayer Practice:	Practice of the presence of God
Schedule:	Morning contemplation
	Lauds
	Breakfast
	[Time for prayer, work, sacred reading]
	Lunch
	[Time for prayer, work, sacred reading]
	Vespers
	Evening contemplation
	Dinner
	[Time for recreation]
	Compline

Day Two

Theme:	Gestation
Prayer:	Petition
Prayer Practice:	The Jesus Prayer
Schedule:	Same as day one

Day Three

Theme:	Resurrection
Prayer:	Adoration and praise
Prayer Practice:	The Lord's Prayer
Schedule:	Same as day one

walked halfway up the flagstone path to the front door, then turned around and retreated to my car. There I was seized with disgust at my cowardice and turned back again. Halfway up, and again I reversed. I must have spun around five or six times; any monks watching from within might have thought me an eccentric Sufi, practicing his whirls in the Massachusetts snow. Finally, I steeled myself and knocked. A beaming man, his white robe dazzling against his coconut-brown skin, opened the door. He ushered me in, and my life changed forever.

This comic episode drives home a simple truth: Anxieties may be normal, but we cannot let them rule. We must banish from our minds all anticipation, all fear, all imagination about what we might encounter. The key is trust. Trust the retreat, trust the men and women who have refined these practices over the course of centuries. Trust God, who ceaselessly guards our welfare.

I would like to suggest that before going to sleep tonight, you slip on a jacket and walk out under the stars. These far-off furnaces began to blaze long before your birth, and they will continue to burn long after your death. The stars are emblems of eternity, semaphores of God. As their light spills down on you, remember who you are. Remember who you wish to be. Remember why you have chosen to go on retreat. Remember the holy men and women who proceeded you in this movement toward the desert, and who will accompany you along the way: Remember the saints, the apostles, Christ himself. Remember his call of love, which never ends.

> O Lord of Life, fountain of all creation,
> You breathe and the world begins.
> You shape us from clay,
> You hold us in your hand.
> Bring us into your heart.

Guide us on this retreat we are about to begin,
As we place ourselves wholly into your loving care.
Give us the wisdom, the knowledge, the strength we seek.
Give us what you will.

Chapter Four

DAY ONE

BEGINNING THE DAY

W e start each day with thirty minutes of contemplative prayer, a silent sitting meditation during which we open ourselves to God's presence. Contemplative prayer lies at the heart of monastic practice. Through it, we invite God to catalyze our being. In effect, contemplative prayer marks a retreat within our retreat, a withdrawal into the Holy of Holies, whose doors open only when we reach a state of profound recollection and receptivity. This practice requires no words, no implements, no ritual. On the contrary, in contemplative prayer we strip naked before God.

The Christian tradition abounds in great masters of contemplation, from John the Evangelist at the end of the first century to the Saharan hermit Charles de Foucauld in the twentieth. But the prototype of all Christian contemplatives remains Mary, sister of Martha:

> Now as they went on their way, he [Jesus] entered a village; and a woman called Martha received him into her house. And she had a sister named Mary, who sat at the Lord's feet and listened to his teaching. But Martha was distracted with much serving;

and she went to him and said, "Lord, do you not care that my sister has left me to serve alone? Tell her then to help me." But the Lord answered her, "Martha, Martha, you are anxious and troubled about many things; one thing is needful. Mary has chosen the good portion, which shall not be taken away from her.

(Luke 10:38–42, RSV)

We too can begin our day by choosing the "good portion," the "one thing needful." In Mary's gesture, we see the essential simplicity of contemplative prayer, for it consists in nothing other than this: putting aside our anxieties and troubles in order to sit at God's feet. A few people may harbor fears that contemplation is reserved for spiritual adepts, a belief unfortunately fostered at various times in the history of the Church. But as the Gospel story suggests, contemplation—like retreat itself—is meant for all, beginning or advanced. We need have no worries on that account.

What really takes place during contemplative prayer? Some saints speak of divine energies or rays of darkness or infused graces. Others liken the process to divine illumination, in which God, the sun of our spiritual cosmos, renews creation in the light of love, the same light that gave it birth:

For it is the God who said, "Let light shine out of darkness," who has shone in our hearts to give the light of the knowledge of the glory of God in the face of Jesus Christ. *(2 Corinthians 4:6)*

Perhaps the best definition comes from Gregory the Great, who describes contemplation as "resting in God." Once immersed in contemplative prayer, our task is to await God, as humbly and simply and quietly as possible. Martha's bustle has no place here. We sit and we wait. That is all. We may hope for immediate results; we may even dream of attaining the highest stages of contemplative prayer, which the great Spanish Carmelite saints depict as "mystical marriage" or "mystical union" with God. But we cannot possibly measure the manner or means of God's work within us. Don't be discouraged if there seems to be no evidence of change. God's activity is often invisible, unfolding at levels far below and above conscious thought, initiating a transformation whose results may become apparent only far in the future, perhaps at the moment of death.

THE METHOD OF CONTEMPLATIVE PRAYER

It is best to enter into contemplative prayer soon after arising for the day, and certainly before breakfast. A glass of orange juice will do no harm, but more substantial food may weigh down the body and interfere with the subtle interplay of energies that takes place during contemplation.

Begin by sitting in a comfortable position on chair, *zafu,* or *seiza* bench. Arms should be relaxed, one hand cupped lightly in the other, palms up. The spine must be erect. To achieve this, imagine that a string has been attached to the top of your head and is gently pulling you upward. This motion straightens and relaxes the spinal column. Not only will you find this position comfortable—it can be sustained for hours, if necessary, without undue muscular strain—but it carries spiritual significance as well, for only an erect posture befits our stature as children of God, "God's vice-regents on earth," as the Koran puts it. (We hear, in common speech, echoes of the spiritual symbolism of verticality in such terms as "moral uprightness" or "rectitude.")

Once we have established a stable, upright position, a brief relaxation exercise will help prepare us for contemplative prayer. Imagine that a warm, nourishing light is shining onto the top of your head. The light softly massages your scalp, erasing all tensions and anxieties. Very slowly, the light moves down to the forehead, smoothing all the little muscles, melting away the tightness. The light caresses the skin with infinite gentleness. Slowly it glides down to your face, washing the tension from eyes, lips, and jaw. Let the light bathe your neck and shoulders, let it take away the strain in arms, wrists, hands. The light floods your chest with warm radiance. It flows down to your solar plexus, where you might discover a tight knot of muscular and emotional tension. Never mind; the warm light washes this away as well. Let the light pass down your groin area, your legs, and onto your feet, caressing as it goes.

Follow this procedure slowly and carefully. When you are finished, no muscular or nervous tension should remain.

After the initial relaxation exercise has been completed, return your attention to your chest. Turn inward and enter the temple of your heart. Sit in silence and stillness, remembering why you are here.

Breathe slowly, in a natural, relaxed manner. In the Christian tradition, breath represents much more than the physiological process of respiration. It is the atmosphere in which we live, the winds that stir our planet, and the Holy Spirit, giver of life. During contemplative prayer, says John of the Cross, Creator and creature breathe with the same breath. Breath anchors our prayer. If in the midst of your contemplation you suddenly find yourself miles away from prayer, remembering yesterday's dinner or last week's flirtation, don't be concerned. Simply return to your breathing. Let its rhythm steady you and transport you inward, to begin again your silent vigil. An ancient saying reminds us that "If we take one step, God will take ten thousand." Our only task is to make that first step, to cross the threshold into the sacred chamber, there to await the presence of God.

After thirty minutes, our contemplation ends. We leave the prayer as gently as we entered it. The transition back to ordinary consciousness can be a time of fertile discovery: How can I retain the balance, the tranquility, the sense of wonder that I knew during contemplative prayer? Learn the "taste" of this final moment of prayer, just before the world invades with all its pricks and proddings.

FIRST ADVENTURES

Once we have finished our contemplative prayer, we may want to explore our surroundings. We have oriented ourselves inwardly, pointing our soul's compass toward the true north of God; now it is time to do the same with our environment. In a strange location, say a monastic guest house or an isolated cabin, we instinctively feel the need for such exploration. But I urge it even if the retreat takes place at home; for most people know much less about their homes than they think.

Orientation can take many forms. For some aboriginal peoples, it entails locating the four cardinal directions. Huichol Indians on the sacred peyote hunt always begin in this way and recheck their orientation throughout the pilgrimage, to know where they stand in relation to the cosmos and to ensure proper alignment with those forces that stream toward earth from all directions and all levels of creation. In the Christian tradition, too, one finds orientation according to the compass; in Gothic cathedrals, for instance, the main entrance faces west and the altar stands to the east.

But orientation involves more than finding one's little place in the larger universe; it also means finding the larger universe in one's little place. Once, during a retreat at a lovely Quaker farmstead in rural Massachusetts, I wound up in a cabin that had no electricity. As the sun fell, it suddenly dawned on me that I would soon be wandering in pitch blackness, for I had neglected to pack a flashlight or candles (so much for careful planning). That evening, I banged elbows and shins more times than I care to remember as I floundered around from kitchen to bedroom to outhouse. The next morning, I determined to become friends with my environment. I spent the next few hours getting to know each decrepit stick of furniture, each corner of the blackened stove, every sagging rafter and cracked windowpane.

As the cabin and I became acquainted, I warmed toward it: This, I realized, was the space set aside for me on my mission to the interior of the heart. I began to love this little cabin, and I began to see in its crude pine walls and blotchy floor the outlines of grace. For most of us, God does not speak in abstract reasoning but in the concrete friction and knocks of everyday life. In the rough boards of this cabin, in my stinging elbows and bruised knees, I began to sense God's presence, benevolent and amused. During my explorations of my world, I found a spider, too: an orange-and-black little fellow living on a frayed web beneath the sink. This spider became a companion for me during my adventures. I never spoke to him, nor he to me, but during my meditations I was often aware of his presence: silent, solitary, industrious in his own spiderly way, on permanent retreat from the great pine forests outside our walls, a hermit of the animal world.

TODAY'S THEME: DETACHMENT, OR DEATH

The theme for today is surrender, detachment, or—not to beat around the bush—that most frightening of words, death. But why speak of dying at the beginning of retreat? Haven't we sequestered ourselves in search of renewal, rebirth, the dawn of new possibilities? Yes, and for just that reason, death must play its part. To see why, let us consider the astonishing case of the blind Frenchman Jacques Lusseyran.

Time: May 3, 1932. Place: a schoolroom in Paris, France. The bell sounds for recess; in the ensuing commotion, a seven-year-old boy falls against a desk, smashing his spectacles, driving glass splinters into his right eye. The eye goes blind forever; a few days later, the second eye follows suit, through "sympathetic ophthalmia." A tragedy? Let us hear how Lusseyran himself evaluates the aftermath of this event that utterly changed his life: "Since the day I went blind I have never been unhappy."[1]

The mind reels. How can this be? Lusseyran admits that at first he met our expectations. He seethed with horror at this involuntary and permanent retreat from the world of sight. He hated his blindness, despised his weakness, despaired over his future. Then one day, "and it was not long in coming," the truth dawned on him: "I realized that I was looking in the wrong way. . . . I was looking too far off, and too much on the surface of things."[2] Out of necessity, the little boy learned to see in a new way:

> I began to look. . . at a world closer to myself, looking from an inner place to one further within, instead of clinging to the movement of sight toward the world outside.
>
> Immediately the substance of the universe drew together, redefined and peopled itself anew. I was aware of a radiance emanating from a place I knew nothing about, a place which might as well have been outside me as within. But radiance was there, or, to put it more precisely, light.[3]

In time, this revelation—no other word seems appropriate—carried Lusseyran into extraordinary adventures both inner and outer. His senses burst into magnificent new life: He heard a Bach concerto as a cascade of colors; he handled an apple and "I didn't even know whether I was touching it or it was touching me. As I became part of the apple, the apple became part of me. And that was how I came to understand the existence of things."[4]

Less than a decade later, Nazi tanks rolled over France. In response, Lusseyran founded—at the age of sixteen!—the Volunteers of Liberty, one of the most important of the underground resistance groups. His ability to judge character had become so acute that he took on the critical job of screening all recruits. By discerning minute fluctuations in the human voice—the signal of moral rot—he could sniff out a traitor instantly. Just once he disregarded the promptings of his intuition. The error landed him in Buchenwald, where the blind man became the light of the camp, as he explains:

> Light had become a substance within me. It broke into my cage, pushed by a force a thousand times stronger than I. . . . there was one thing left which I could do: not refuse God's help, the breath he was blowing upon me. . . . I could try to show other people how to go about holding on to life. I could turn toward them the flow of light and joy which had grown so abundant in me. From that time on they stopped stealing my bread or my soup. It never happened again. Often my comrades would wake me up in the night and take me to comfort someone, sometimes a long way off in another block.
>
> Almost everyone forgot I was a student. I became "the blind Frenchman." For many, I was just "the man who didn't die."[5]

How can we sum up this extraordinary story? Forced into exile from the world of sight, from all the visual cues and codes that we take so much for granted, Lusseyran discovered a new language, that of the heart. He learned "with absolute certainty that everything in the world was a sign of something else." "Some people would say I had faith," he writes, "and how should I not have it in the presence of the marvel which kept renewing itself?"[6]

I have recounted Jacques Lusseyran's story in depth, because in it we see the spiritual meaning of death: death as the shedding of old skin that binds us, the shucking of old habits that blind us, death as the prelude to spiritual rebirth. Said Jesus to Nicodemus, "Truly, truly, I say to you, unless one is born anew, he cannot see the kingdom of God" (John 3:3, RSV).

TODAY'S PROMISE: STABILITY

On this first day of retreat, as we plunge into the ocean of spiritual renewal, we might be wracked with anxiety or fear at the immensity of our task. We do well to remember that we have not been cast adrift. We anchor ourselves in God, and we begin to move on his abiding currents. Benedictines drop anchor by making a special promise of stability, vowing themselves for life to the monastery where they received their spiritual formation. This pledge of outward stability holds an inner meaning as well. Through stability of place, the monk or nun seeks stability of heart—an always more profound love of the spiritual life, accompanied by the courage to persevere on the monastic path.

These ambitions demand energy, sometimes great amounts of it. Although people take stability to imply standing still, or even lassitude, nothing could be further from the truth. In fact, when not immersed in contemplative prayer or seated in the choir for Mass or the Divine Office, monks and nuns pitch into their work with a gusto that puts the ant and bee to shame. In a sense, this ceaseless striving rules the inner life as well, at least amongst those monks and nuns whom I have met; thus Benedict in the *Rule* speaks of "hastening on to the perfection of monastic life" (*RB* 73). We find this dynamic activity in the story of Jacques Lusseyran as well. Once on the inner path, Lusseyran never idled; to do so would have been to blind himself again, this time willingly. Instead, he pressed onward, molding his inward vision into a tool for others as well as himself. Yet Lusseyran and the Benedictines have this in common:

Underneath the furious enterprise lies a center of absolute stillness, the eye of the hurricane, where they rest in the presence
of God. In this silent cathedral deep within the heart, all on
the spiritual path find at last true stability, a home forever.
Throughout this day, in all the activities detailed below, we
will discover the meaning of stability for ourselves, and reap its
rewards.

DIVINE OFFICE

Legend has it that Immanuel Kant kept so strict a daily routine that the housewives of Königsberg set their clocks by his
morning constitutional. But we mustn't confuse outward reg-
ularity with lack of inner life; for Kant gave the world a
philosophical system of dazzling originality and moral force.
We find the same in the life of Bach: a man of surpassing or-
dinariness who, from the stability of his dull bourgeois life,
composed the greatest religious music that the world has ever
known.

So it is in the monastery as well. The regular round of private and communal prayer, sacred reading, and manual labor
renewed every day through the year, across the decades, down
the centuries, has become the heartbeat of monasticism, the
rhythmic expression of its vital life. As I said in chapter 2, this
life revolves around the Divine Office. The Office always takes
precedence; when the bell sounds the Hour, monk or nun
drops whatever work is at hand and hastens to the chapel.
Here the entire community offers itself to God and to the
world, for whose welfare it prays. Through our own efforts at
the *opus Dei,* however tentative, feeble, or fumbling they may
be, we too share in this great endeavor and enjoy some measure of the stability that it brings.

For the sake of both simplicity and serenity, as I explained in chapter 2, we will cut back on the daily regime (no one should spend the entire retreat wrestling with chant). We will retain the three most important Hours:

> Lauds, or Morning Office (prayed before breakfast)
> Vespers, or Evening Office (prayed before dinner)
> Compline, or Night Office (prayed before retiring for the night)

In the choice of texts for the Divine Office, we adhere strictly to custom. The words for Friday, the first day of our retreat, are the same as those chanted on Friday in Benedictine monasteries throughout the world. The same applies for Saturday and Sunday. Nothing has been added; abbreviations occur only when necessary.

The Hours retain the same structure each day, a great aid in the quest for stability. The template is:

Lauds (Morning Office)

> Introductory prayer
> Morning psalm
> Old Testament canticle
> Psalm of praise
> Scripture reading
> Silent prayer
> Gospel Canticle of Zechariah
> The Lord's Prayer
> Concluding prayer
> Blessing

Vespers (Evening Office)

- Introductory prayer
- Psalm
- Psalm
- New Testament canticle
- Scripture reading
- Silent prayer
- Gospel Canticle of Mary
- The Lord's Prayer
- Concluding prayer
- Blessing

Compline (Night Office)

- Introductory prayer
- Examination of conscience
- Psalm
- Scripture reading
- Silent prayer
- Gospel canticle
- Concluding prayer
- Blessing
- Salve Regina

Before we begin the *opus Dei,* we must address an important question: how to recite the psalms, canticles, readings, and prayers that constitute each Hour. Benedict offers a modicum of advice, telling us that the Hours should be prayed "with humility, seriousness, and reverence" (*RB* 47). Each of these qualifiers carries its own cargo of meaning. "Seriousness" suggests that we recite the text while holding in mind its sacred character; "reverence" that we do so while remaining alert to the presence of God, who listens to our every syllable and silence; "humility," that we do so while remembering our smallness and God's greatness. Needless to say, we can hardly keep these ideas in mind at all times as we pray; to do so would guarantee distraction (like thinking about the location of letters on a keyboard while trying to type). Something else is needed, some ingredient that will bring along with it the requisite humility, gravity, and reverence.

In Christian monasticism, this element is found in the disposition, or inner posture, of the monk or nun in prayer. We may describe it as "relaxed attention," or conversely, as "active passivity," that state of being that allows a free exchange of love between monk and God, without ego getting in the way. This disposition can be ours as well. We need to step aside and let the prayer pass unimpeded from our hearts to God and back again. Many people wonder how to attain this state of spiritual transparency; perhaps the simplest suggestion would be to say the Hour with grace. Of course, the word "grace" packs a plethora of meanings, some of them of enormous theological complexity. Keep it simple: Picture a ballerina *en pointe,* a priest elevating the Host, a bride or groom walking to the altar. In the bearing of each, we glimpse what is meant in this context by grace, the marriage of humility, gravity, and reverence.

My young son, John, often breaks into song when he dives into a beloved hobby, such as rearranging his action figures into new ranks and files. Singing expresses joy, at least for human beings, birds, and angels. However, many of us will shy away from singing the Divine Office, no matter how blissful we feel. This is as it should be; to be done with any chance of success, Gregorian chant demands years of vocal training and a specialized knowledge of medieval neumes. Instead of embarrassing ourselves and the great tradition in which we participate, I suggest that we recite the Hours out loud, quietly but firmly. Let me repeat: out loud. This is essential. Vocalization gives to us—and summons from us—vast resources unknown in silent reading. We drench ourselves in the exquisite beauty of psalm and canticle, and we pour out this beauty upon the world. By sounding the words, we take a stand: We declare ourselves to God with our bodies as well as our minds.

Most of us, I suspect, will undertake this retreat alone, and therefore will miss the experience of the communal Divine Office. Yet our solitude holds certain advantages. Friedrich Nietzsche observed that "when we talk in company we lose our unique tone of voice." On retreat, we talk by ourselves; or more precisely, we engage in a private conversation one-on-one with God. As a result, the "unique tone of voice" belonging to each of us has a chance to sound forth. However, this requires special care. The words must be enunciated as attentively as possible, with the sound originating in the chest rather than the larynx; this will ensure the vocal resonance worthy of sacred texts.

Posture plays its part in the Divine Office as well. The words can be recited sitting or standing; in either case, as with contemplative prayer, it is essential that the spine be erect, the head carefully balanced atop the spinal column. Muscular tension should be at a minimum; we offer to God not only our voices but our entire bodies. Try to remember the feeling of profound recollection that you knew during the depths of contemplative prayer, and work to recapture that state during the *opus Dei*. However, don't despair if this seems impossible. I have said the Hours under many circumstances: in distress, in high dudgeon, while dizzy with joy; and I have found that none of this matters much. Only the words matter. If we empty ourselves of all extraneous business, we will be filled only with prayer, and with the divine love that courses through the prayer, and all will be well in the praying.

We stand or sit (the choice is ours) through most of the Divine Office, but one other position comes into play now and then. To the conclusion of every psalm or canticle, monastic tradition appends a hymn of praise to God, known as the doxology:

> Glory be to the Father and to the Son and to the Holy Spirit, as it was in the beginning, is now, and ever shall be, world without end, Amen.

In this acclamation, we acknowledge God's glory (Greek *doxa*, Hebrew *kabod*), which Jewish and early Christian tradition understood as a radiant royal presence, and we bear witness to the traditional Trinitarian understanding of God as three-persons-in-one, a self-reflective community of love. While reciting the doxology, we bow deeply from the waist. Zen monks and nuns bow to their *roshi,* knights to their ladies, peacocks to their peahens. We find this gesture everywhere on earth, enclosing in its simple form a wealth of meanings, including obeisance, humility, service, and gratitude. The bow has become my favorite moment during the Divine Office, and I hope that you will relish it as well.

One note of caution as we start the *opus Dei:* Some of the passages may be startling in their ferocity. Bear in mind that these psalms and canticles were composed in a world far removed from our own. War, plague, famine, and other terrors ruled the day. Death knocked nightly at the door of neighbor, relative—or oneself. For the suffering people, God became, as the psalmist says, "our refuge and our strength." Conditions have changed—although perhaps not so much as we may like—but the power and value of this venerable tradition remain intact. Recite the scriptures with attention, and you will surely encounter, as did the ancient Israelites, the glory and tenderness of God.

THE DIVINE OFFICE FOR FRIDAY

Lauds

INTRODUCTORY PRAYER

Lord, Open my lips, and my mouth will proclaim your praise.

(Bow) Glory be to the Father, and to the Son, and to the Holy Spirit. As it was in the beginning, is now, and ever shall be, world without end, Amen.

MORNING PSALM (PSALM 119:145–49)

With my whole heart I cry; answer me, O Lord.
> I will keep your statutes.
I cry to you; save me,
> that I may observe your decrees.
I rise before dawn and cry for help;
> I put my hope in your words.
My eyes are awake before each watch of the night,
> that I may meditate on your promise.
In your steadfast love hear my voice;
> O Lord, in your justice preserve my life.

(Bow) Glory be . . .

OLD TESTAMENT CANTICLE (ISAIAH 45:15–19)

Truly, you are a God who hides himself,
> O God of Israel, the Savior.

All of them are put to shame and confounded,
   the makers of idols go in confusion together.
But Israel is saved by the Lord
   with everlasting salvation;
you shall not be put to shame or confounded
   to all eternity.

For thus says the Lord,
who created the heavens
   (he is God!),
who formed the earth and made it
   (he established it;
he did not create it a chaos,
   he formed it to be inhabited!)
I am the Lord, and there is no other.
I did not speak in secret,
   in a land of darkness;
I did not say to the offspring of Jacob,
   "Seek me in chaos."
I the Lord speak the truth,
   I declare what is right.

   (Bow) Glory be . . .

PSALM OF PRAISE (PSALM 100)

   Make a joyful noise to the Lord, all the earth.
      Worship the Lord with gladness;
      come into his presence with singing.

   Know that the Lord is God.
      It is he that made us, and we are his;
   . we are his people, and the sheep of his pasture.

Enter his gates with thanksgiving, and his courts
   with praise.
Give thanks to him, bless his name.
For the Lord is good;
   his steadfast love endures forever,
   and his faithfulness to all generations.

(Bow) Glory be . . .

SCRIPTURE READING (EPHESIANS 4:29–32)

Let no evil come out of your mouths, but only what is useful for building up, as there is need, so that your words
may give grace to those who hear. And do not grieve the
Holy Spirit of God, with which you were marked with a
seal for the day of redemption. Put away from you all bitterness and wrath and anger and wrangling and slander,
together with all malice, and be kind to one another, ten-
derhearted, forgiving one another, as God in Christ has
forgiven you.

SILENT PRAYER

(For a few minutes, we pray to God in silence and stillness. Our prayer may take whatever form we feel is needful at the moment: thanksgiving, petition, praise,
adoration.)

GOSPEL CANTICLE OF ZECHARIAH (LUKE 1:68–79)

Blessed be the Lord God of Israel,
   for he has looked favorably on his people and
      redeemed them.
He has raised up a mighty savior for us
   in the house of his servant David,

as he spoke through the mouth of his holy prophets
   from of old,
      that we would be saved from our enemies and
      from the hand of all who hate us.
Thus he has shown the mercy promised to our
   ancestors,
      and has remembered his holy covenant,
the oath that he swore to our ancestor Abraham,
   to grant us that we, being rescued from the hands
   of our enemies,
might serve him without fear, in holiness and
   righteousness before him all our days.
And you, child, will be called the prophet of the Most
   High;
      for you will go before the Lord to prepare his
      ways,
to give knowledge of salvation to his people
   by the forgiveness of their sins.
By the tender mercy of our God,
   the dawn from on high will break upon us,
to give light to those who sit in darkness and in the
   shadow of death,
      to guide our feet into the way of peace.

(Bow) Glory be . . .

THE LORD'S PRAYER

   Our Father, who art in heaven,
      hallowed be thy name.
   Thy kingdom come, thy will be done,
      On earth as it is in heaven.
   Give us this day our daily bread,

and forgive us our trespasses,
as we forgive those who trespass against us.
And lead us not into temptation,
but deliver us from evil.

CONCLUDING PRAYER

We ask this through Jesus Christ, your Son, who lives and reigns with you and the Holy Spirit, one God forever and ever, Amen.

BLESSING

May the Lord God bless us, guide us, guard us from evil, and bring us to life eternal, Amen.

Vespers

INTRODUCTORY PRAYER

God come to my assistance, Lord make haste to help me.

(Bow) Glory be . . .

PSALM (PSALM 116:1–7)

I love the Lord, because he has heard
my voice and my supplications.
Because he inclined his ear to me,
therefore I will call on him as long as I live.
The snares of death encompassed me;
the pangs of Sheol laid hold on me;
I suffered distress and anguish.
Then I called on the name of the Lord:
"O Lord, I pray, save my life!"

Gracious is the Lord, and righteous;
our God is merciful.
The Lord protects the simple;

when I was brought low, he saved me.
Return, O my soul, to your rest,
for the Lord has dealt bountifully with you.

(Bow) Glory be . . .

PSALM (PSALM 121)

I lift up my eyes to the hills—
from where will my help come?
My help comes from the Lord,
who made heaven and earth.

He will not let your foot be moved;
he who keeps you will not slumber.
He who keeps Israel
will neither slumber nor sleep.

The Lord is your keeper;
the Lord is your shade at your right hand.
The sun shall not strike you by day,
nor the moon by night.

The Lord will keep you from all evil;
he will keep your life.
The Lord will keep
your going out and your coming in
from this time on and forevermore.

(Bow) Glory be . . .

NEW TESTAMENT CANTICLE (REVELATION 15:3–4)

Great and amazing are your deeds,
Lord God the Almighty!
Just and true are your ways,
King of the nations!

Lord, who will not fear
   and glorify your name?
For you alone are holy.
   All nations will come
   and worship before you,
for your judgments have been revealed.

(Bow) Glory be . . .

SCRIPTURE READING (JAMES 1:2–4)

My brothers and sisters, whenever you face trials of any
kind, consider it nothing but joy, because you know that
the testing of your faith produces endurance; and let endurance have its full effect, so that you may be mature and
complete, lacking in nothing.

SILENT PRAYER

GOSPEL CANTICLE OF MARY (LUKE 1:46–55)

My soul magnifies the Lord,
   and my spirit rejoices in God my Savior,
for he has looked with favor on the lowliness of his
      servant.
   Surely, from now on all generations will call me
      blessed;
for the Mighty One has done great things for me,
   and holy is his name.
His mercy is for those who fear him
   from generation to generation.
He has shown strength with his arm;
   he has scattered the proud in the thoughts of their
      hearts.
He has brought down the powerful from their
      thrones,

and lifted up the lowly;
    he has filled the hungry with good things,
        and sent the rich away empty.
He has helped his servant Israel,
    in remembrance of his mercy,
according to the promise he made to our ancestors,
    to Abraham and to his descendants forever.

(Bow) Glory be . . .

THE LORD'S PRAYER

CONCLUDING PRAYER

We ask this through Jesus Christ, your Son, who lives and
reigns with you and the Holy Spirit, one God forever and
ever, Amen.

BLESSING

May the Lord God bless us, guide us, guard us from evil,
and bring us to life eternal, Amen.

Compline

INTRODUCTORY PRAYER

God, come to my assistance; Lord, make haste to help me.

(Bow) Glory be . . .

EXAMINATION OF CONSCIENCE

(For a few moments, we think back over the day, paying
particular attention to any failures in our behavior toward
ourselves or others. Do we see anything that troubles us in
our thoughts or actions? We resolve, simply and gently, to
do our best tomorrow.)

PSALM (PSALM 86:1–7)

Incline your ear, O Lord, and answer me,
    for I am poor and needy.
Preserve my life, for I am devoted to you;
    save your servant who trusts in you.
You are my God; be gracious to me, O Lord.
    for to you do I cry all day long.
Gladden the soul of your servant,
    for to you, O Lord, I lift up my soul.
For you, O Lord, are good and forgiving,
    abounding in steadfast love to all who call on you.
Give ear, O Lord, to my prayer;
    listen to my cry of supplication.
In the day of my trouble I call on you,
    for you will answer me.

(Bow) Glory be . . .

SCRIPTURE READING (1 CORINTHIANS 13:1–7)

If I speak in the tongues of mortals and of angels, but do not have love, I am a noisy gong or a clanging cymbal. And if I have prophetic powers, and understand all mysteries and all knowledge, and if I have all faith, so as to remove mountains, but do not have love, I am nothing. If I give away all my possessions, and if I hand over my body so that I may boast, but do not have love, I gain nothing.

Love is patient; love is kind; love is not envious or boastful or arrogant or rude. It does not insist on its own way; it is not irritable or resentful; it does not rejoice in wrongdoing, but rejoices in the truth. It bears all things, believes all things, hopes all things, endures all things.

The Recollected Heart

SILENT PRAYER

GOSPEL CANTICLE (LUKE 2:29–32)

Master, now you are dismissing your servant in
    peace,
    according to your word;
for my eyes have seen your salvation,
    which you have prepared in the presence of all
    peoples,
a light for revelation to the Gentiles
    and for glory to your people Israel.

(Bow) Glory be . . .

CONCLUDING PRAYER

We pray to you Lord, let your holy angels watch over us
and let your love be with us always, through Christ our
Lord, Amen.

BLESSING

May God grant us a peaceful night, a peaceful death, and
perfect peace hereafter.

SALVE REGINA

(a prayer to the Blessed Virgin Mary)

Hail holy Queen, mother of mercy,
    our life, our sweetness, and our hope.
To you do we cry,
    poor banished children of Eve.
To you do we send up our sighs,
    mourning and weeping in this valley of tears.
Turn then, O most gracious advocate,
    your merciful eyes toward us.

And after this, our exile,
show to us the blessed fruit of your womb, Jesus.
O clement, O loving, O sweet Virgin Mary.

(The Great Silence descends, not to be broken until the next morning.)

Sacred Reading for Today

I once knew a woman who purchased all her clothes through mail-order catalogues. She adored shopping, and every week a new set of packages tumbled across her doorstep. Whenever I stopped by for a visit, I found her sofa and easy chairs festooned with dresses, blouses, skirts, and sweaters, tags intact. A few other items always lay close at hand: tape, cord, packing boxes, and stamps. For my friend had a little secret: She knew ahead of time that few of the clothes would fit (her postage bills must have been enormous). The source of her clairvoyance? She never ordered to match her current size, but to conform to an ideal shape, the slim self she had once been and planned to be again.

As with clothes, so with prayer. There's no point in struggling with sacred texts that just won't fit. This doesn't mean, of course, that we should settle for polyester; merely that different words suit different people. This must be borne in mind when selecting the reading material for *lectio divina*. For each day of our retreat, I will suggest one passage drawn from the New Testament and based on the theme of the day (I won't analyze the text for you, for *lectio divina* is another way that God speaks to each of use alone). Please don't feel bound by my selection. Whatever reading brings you closer to God constitutes authentic *lectio divina*. Rather than read snippets of scripture, you might want to study an entire gospel or epistle during the course of the retreat. Nor should you feel compelled to read at a specific time; God awaits you always. Whatever you read and whenever you read it, be sure to proceed slowly, masticating each sentence (as medieval monks would say) in order to extract its full nutrition. Today's suggestion for *lectio divina* is the parable of the sower: Matthew 13:1–23, Mark 4:1–25, or Luke 8:4–18.

MANUAL LABOR FOR TODAY

Henry Thoreau's activities at Walden Pond suggest—but by no means exhaust—the range of manual labor suitable for retreat: He erected a cabin, planted trees, cultivated beans, jawed with neighbors, measured snowdrifts, plumbed the pond's bottom, and hiked more often than his legend allows to the center of Concord. The same options apply to our time alone. Some of us may work at a craft, perhaps cooking, sewing, or weaving. Others prefer sweatier tasks: hoeing a garden, uprooting weeds, cleaning a chimney, repainting a shed. All these jobs fit perfectly with retreat, for they keep our hands occupied while our mind rests in God.

I advise you, however, to avoid a third category of work: the fine arts, such as composing a painting, a sonata, or a poem. No one, I hope, frowns on these activities per se. They are monastic to the core. Benedictines in particular have been acclaimed for the high quality of their music, literature, and scholarship. However, such activities demand fierce concentration, often at the expense of recollection (notice how many great artists—Picasso, Beethoven, Byron, for example—are notorious for their turbulent lives). Because of this, fine arts usually fall to the hands of older monks and nuns, who have already established a solid foundation of contemplation and prayer. As beginners, we must follow their lead, putting aside anything that will deflect us from our aim. Save the fine arts for another day.

Apart from this caveat, it scarcely matters what manual work you choose. If nothing else appeals, get on your hands and knees and scrub the decks. From Jerusalem to Japan, dirt symbolizes confusion, obscuration, wandering off the path, while cleanliness, by contrast, signifies truth—and the ability to perceive it. The Psalter says, "Who shall ascend the hill of the Lord? And who shall stand in his holy place? Those who have clean hands and pure hearts" (Psalm 24:3–4).

However you choose to employ your hands, whether hammering a nail, weaving a tapestry, or washing a wall, remember that your task serves two ends. One is material and self-evident: By hammering the nail, you build the house. The second is spiritual and elusive, for manual labor builds up the inner world as well. To drive a nail is no mean accomplishment, but to drive a nail while in a state of prayer elevates one to another plane entirely. "Well then," you might ask, "how do I do this? I've cursed more than once while hammering, but never yet prayed." But there's nothing mysterious about work-in-prayer. The key consists in expanding one's attention, lending part of it to God while the rest occupies itself with the task at hand. We do something akin to this whenever we talk while driving, or sing while bathing, or eat a hot dog while watching the ball game. Notice that of these paired actions, one is predominately physical, the other predominately mental. Tackling two mental tasks at once—say, counting forward and backward at the same time—is bound to short-circuit. For just this reason, our labor on retreat must be manual, leaving our minds free to turn to God. Joining sweat and prayer, we sanctify our activities; we become not only apprentice carpenters or potters or cooks, but apprentice saints as well.

For this reason alone, we should learn to rejoice in our mistakes. We haven't set out to win the blue ribbon at the local 4-H, but to win a truer way of life. I remember an incident that took place during a group retreat about ten years ago. A team of five or six people had assigned themselves the task of painting a house interior. One of the young men present, whom we will call Sam—a scholar more accustomed to scraping meaning from ancient parchment than old paint from walls—volunteered to prep and paint the staircase. For hours he scratched away at the flaking old paint, stirring up clouds of plaster dust in the process. Soon a greasy film covered every surface in sight, including Sam, his coworkers, and the stairs. Finally, Sam pronounced his prep work done and dashed upstairs to grab the paint. As he came down again, a five-gallon can of white latex in hand, he slipped on the plaster dust. I shall never forget the look on his face—a mix of bewilderment, horror, and awe—nor the graceful arc made by the paint as it poured through the air, like a thick white ocean wave, before splashing across walls, banister, risers, floor, and the heads of the assembled painting team. It took us most of the day to clean up the mess.

From one perspective, Sam's tumble amounted to a perfect fiasco. But later he confided in me—and he meant it—that spilling the paint was "one of the best things that had ever happened" to him. Why? In part, Sam said, because he prided himself on being a meticulous, mistake-free worker; and when the accident took place, he saw his inattention and vanity literally broadcast across the room. "Every time I climb those stairs," he said, "I'll remember who I really am." In part, too, he traced his good feelings to the cleanup, in which everyone took part, a concrete expression of the solidarity that develops on retreat. And then again, he added, there was a third reason,

perhaps the best: We looked hilarious with white paint stream-
ing down our faces. No doubt we did; Sam's mistake deflated a
bit of our own self-importance as well.

TODAYS'S PRAYER PRACTICE:
PRACTICING THE PRESENCE OF GOD

In Andrew Davis's movie *Under Siege,* Steven Seagal plays a
cook on the *U.S.S. Missouri,* a warship slated for mothballs.
When terrorists board the vessel to hijack a brace of nuclear-
tipped missiles, the viewer soon discovers that beneath his
chef's hat, Seagal wears (figuratively speaking) the black cap of
a special Navy operative. Almost single-handedly, our hero
routs the enemy and saves the West from nuclear holocaust. In
this live-action cartoon, we can discern one of the oldest folk-
lore motifs, that of the king in disguise. The theme crops up in
one fairy tale after another: This frog is really a handsome
prince; that tree, a sinuous dryad. Another variation involves
the veiled master, the man or woman of impeccable attain-
ments but unprepossessing—if not downright repellent—
mien. (George Lucas adopted this motif in the *Star Wars*
trilogy for the character of Yoda, the fussy, froglike, 900-year-
old Jedi knight, as did Carlos Castaneda for his irascible Yaqui
sorcerer, Don Juan.)

As astonishing as it sounds, in the religious sphere such
stories sometimes turn out to be true. The most unprepossessing figure may turn out to be a genuis of sanctity. Think of
Thérèse of Lisieux, that giddy teenager cloistered in an out-of-
the-way Carmelite monastery, who became the most cherished
saint of modern times, or Jean Vianney, the Curé d'Ars, whose
spiritual counsel, from his tiny parish in an insignificant French
village, brought solace to millions. Perhaps the most striking
example of hidden sanctity comes to us from seventeenth-

century Paris, in the person of Brother Lawrence of the Resurrection. A self-described "clumsy lummox who broke everything," Brother Lawrence passed his entire adult life in monastic enclosure as a cook and cobbler. He never wrote a book, assembled a circle of pupils, or attained high office. He died as he had lived, in utter obscurity. Yet a handful of his letters and other writings survive to this day, and from them his disciples have culled an extraordinary spiritual method known as "the practice of the presence of God."

The heart of Brother Lawrence's method is this: We find God in the ordinary things of life, in a dusty corridor, a piece of broken china, a stray conversation. We no longer need to climb Sinai to find God; God has descended to earth. In our spiritual childhood, we imagine that only those things specially marked as "sacred"—a shrine, a prayer, a ritual—speak to us of God. But as we mature, we learn that smaller things—a phone call, a passage in a novel—can be vehicles of love, signs of God's presence. As our understanding deepens further, finally it dawns on us that God is everywhere ("the world is charged with the grandeur of God," as Gerard Manley Hopkins so precisely put it).

According to Brother Lawrence, we must consciously strive to greet the world as it comes to us, moment by moment, action by action, person by person. We cease to fret about tomorrow or yesterday; we cease to analyze our behavior; we bid good-bye to daydreams and nightmares; instead, we simply follow the words of the psalmist: "Be still, and know that I am God" (Psalm 46:10). In the following passage, Lawrence describes his method in detail and assures us of its plainness:

> The holiest, most ordinary, and most necessary practice of the spiritual life is that of the presence of God. It is to take delight in and become accustomed to his divine company, speaking humbly and conversing lovingly with him all the time, at every

moment. . . . We must perform all our actions carefully and deliberately, not impulsively or hurriedly, for such would charac-
terize a distracted mind. We must work gently and lovingly
with God.[7]

Lawrence speaks of "conversing lovingly" with God "all
the time, at every moment." Yet who can promise this? How
can we speak to God unceasingly, day and night, while at
the same time maintaining our ordinary activities? What
Lawrence suggests, I believe, is the same inner disposition that
we seek in the Divine Office or contemplative prayer. Perhaps
we can better understand what this asks of us by remembering
the New Testament declaration that "God is love" (1 John 4:8).
God is love, and God resides wherever love is found. If we perform our daily tasks "carefully and deliberately," as Lawrence
recommends—that is to say, if we do them lovingly—then we
will awaken to the presence of the Love within all love. This
idea finds wonderful expression in some great Italian Renais-
sance paintings, such as Giotto's *St. Francis Preaching to the
Birds,* showing the little saint spreading the gospel to a rapt audience of herons, crows, roosters, and other avian catechu-
mens, or Fra Angelico's *Annunciation,* catching the moment
when Mary embraces God's love with her own while proclaiming, "Here I am, the servant of the Lord. Let it be with
me according to your word" (Luke 1:38). In Mary's speech, in
St. Francis's extended arms and open hands, we find just what
Brother Lawrence hopes for us all, a stance of love, compassion, and unconditional acceptance.

The practice of the presence unveils a truth of utmost importance for the spiritual life. Many of us believe God to be remote from our lives, a conviction nourished by the pervasive
loneliness of modern existence, as well as by the disclosures of
science about the vast scale of the universe, the twin abysses of

the atom and the stars. But the great Abrahamic religions—
Judaism, Christianity, and Islam, all offspring of the ancient
Israelites—unite in proclaiming the nearness of God. "God is
closer to you than your own jugular vein," as the Koran has it.
We find this idea concretized in the biblical expression "the
face of God." "Let the light of your face shine on us, O Lord,"
declares the Psalter, a plea echoed by all the prophets. Of
course, the Lord has no face in the literal sense; yet it would be
a great loss to imagine the divinity as faceless, for in this mysterious term, we discern God's tender solicitude. Indeed God
does have a face—brow of power, eyes of mercy, mouth of justice, countenance of love—turned always toward those who
seek the divine presence. Through Brother Lawrence's practice, we learn to recognize this face, we grow to love its con-
tours and lineaments, as we find them reflected in every
moment of our lives.

Throughout the day, then, practice the presence of God.
Don't be discouraged if you slide into distraction; just return to
your efforts, as simply as possible. In order to help you with
this prayer, I would like to suggest that you choose a "sign."
Your sign should be someone or something you will encounter,
in thought if not in the flesh, several times throughout the day.
For example, your sign might be your retreat companion (even
the spider that I befriended on that Quaker retreat), or the on-
off knob on the kitchen stove. Each time you find yourself
face-to-face with your sign—or just thinking of it (or him or
her)—drop your work for a moment, try to recapture the
peace that you knew during contemplative prayer, and then
make an effort to be aware of God's loving presence. You will
find, if you practice diligently, that this exercise will enhance
your openness to God in the same way that isometric exercise
builds muscle tone. As all who hike the spiritual path can

attest, prayer has its muscles as well, and they must be kept limber and strong.

As an additional help in remembering God's presence, pray to your saint for assistance. An excellent occasion for this comes immediately after the morning sitting, before the world has swamped you with its needs. However, anytime will suffice. The simpler the prayer, the better. For instance, you might approach St. Thérèse of Lisieux with the following words: "Dear St. Thérèse, help me to remember God's presence now and always. Amen."

TODAY'S PRAYER THEME: THANKSGIVING

Does it seem strange to offer thanks at the beginning of our retreat? Consider the custom of saying grace: We thank God for our meal before we eat, acknowledging that our steak and potatoes—and we, who eat them—depend on God for very existence:

> O Lord, how manifold are your works!
>   In wisdom you have made them all;
>   the earth is full of your creatures. . . .

> These all look to you
>   to give them their food in due season;
> When you give it to them, they gather it up;
>   when you open your hand, they are filled with good things.
> (Psalm 104:24, 27)

Indeed, our retreat itself—an opportunity denied most human beings—can only be understood as a gift from God. So too for our wish for retreat, our very awareness of spiritual needs and possibilities. God's graciousness toward us began long before we set out for our hermitage; it began, according to scripture, "before the foundation of the world." Our need to give thanks is absolute; it calls, as St. Paul indicates, for an unconditional response:

> Be filled with the spirit, as you sing psalms and hymns and spiritual songs among yourselves, singing and making melody to the Lord in your hearts, giving thanks to God the Father at all times and for everything in the name of our Lord Jesus Christ.
>
> *(Ephesians 5:18–20)*

Note Paul's emphasis on giving thanks "at all times," strikingly similar to Brother Lawrence's "all the time, at every moment." Given the magnitude of God's gifts to us, ceaseless gratitude can be our only response.

As Paul's reference to "psalms and hymns and spiritual songs" indicates, we give thanks first and foremost through the Divine Office. But a second means of thanksgiving, mentioned above, can also play its part. I am thinking of grace before meals, a custom still practiced in homes that retain an awareness of our dependency on divine goodness. Some of my warmest mealtime memories revolve around dinners shared with people of other faiths, where the sound of chanted Tibetan, Japanese, Arabic, or Hebrew filled the air, and God's presence seemed as close as my neighbor's. I would like to assure those unaccustomed to this lovely observance that no better means of thanking God can be found, or ever has been found, than saying grace. Through it, we not only express our gratitude to God for the food upon our table; we also acknowledge the spiritual importance of food. Almost all religions make much of food, for it binds together all beings, animal and vegetable; "Give us this day our daily bread," said Jesus, underscoring its all-abiding importance. Food means more than grain, or wine, or any physical substance: God's love is our daily bread.

Say grace aloud or silently, whichever seems more suitable. You may use a traditional form, such as:

Bless us, O Lord,
and these thy gifts,
which we are about to receive from thy bounty,
through Christ our Lord, Amen.

Or you may design your own grace. In my family, we often use spontaneous forms. John likes to add a boyish spin to his words, giving thanks for the pepperoni topping on the pizza. I suspect that God approves. I fervently hope that saying grace becomes for you a regular practice, at least for the duration of the retreat.

Needless to say, thankfulness extends to more than food. We have all known Pollyannas who avert their eyes from suffering and prattle on about how wonderful life is. When a Pollyanna gives thanks, her words spring from ignorance as much as anything else. But there exists a far more profound thankfulness, that of the man or woman who sees God's graciousness in all events, even in the midst of suffering. Let us remember Jacques Lusseyran, shouting hosannah in his blindness, shedding light in the darkness of Buchenwald. About twenty years ago, I attended a seminar at Harvard University where the Dalai Lama publicly thanked the Chinese Communists for the 1959 invasion that had wrenched him from the Potala Palace and inflicted so much suffering on Tibet. From one perspective, these actions of Lusseyran and the Dalai Lama seem incomprehensible, if not perverse, but in fact they admit a deep spiritual truth. As Lusseyran says, everything is "a sign of something else," of God's providence or of karmic law, depending on one's religious vocabulary. Whatever explanation we choose, the same possibility remains: to turn disaster upside down, through the power of love, into an occasion for giving thanks.

FINISHING THE FIRST DAY

Our daily energy crests around noon. By late afternoon or early evening, muscles and motivations sag; we need a second wind. This holds true for the inner life as well; our attention flags, our prayer practice dwindles to nothing. Sunset is the ideal time to return to contemplation. The more tired you are, the better your prayer will be (as long as you don't topple over or fall asleep): Let your weight settle into the chair, use gravity to cement you to the earth, building an unmovable foundation for your practice. You may find this second session of contemplation to be even more rewarding than the first.

Be sure to sit before dinner. If you must postpone the session until after you eat, postpone it until your food has been digested. During contemplation, your body should do no extraneous work. Once you begin, you will make a remarkable discovery: Right away, you will find yourself in the same immutable stillness that you reached in the morning sitting. It will be as if you have returned to a chamber reserved for contemplation, a room of extraordinary silence and tranquility, a second home.

After dinner, don't return to your work for the day. Evening lends itself to softer modes of activity, like reading, writing, or quiet recreation. Once the sun dips below the horizon, our thinking drops into a new register as well. It slows and deepens; it grows more passive, porous, open to subtle influences. But this happens only if we avoid the artificial stimulation of alcohol, drugs, and television. These things have no place on retreat.

After dark, music comes into its own. Choose well. For our monastic retreat, the most obvious selection, offering both spiritual depth and thematic aptness, will be a Gregorian chant. Meditative works, like Bach's Goldberg Variations or Beethoven's late quartets, also suit. Avoid popular music (show tunes, rock n' roll) that trades in sentimentality, violence, or cheap passion; it will poison your retreat.

———————

During this first day apart, our explorations have ranged from dying to thankfulness, from stability to the practice of the presence. Each of us will be more comfortable with some of these ideas and methods than with others. This is as it should be; only an automaton applauds all that it hears. As we conclude this first day, I would like to pass on to you a hope, a resolution, and a certainty. The hope is that we feel at home on retreat, for retreat means just that: coming home to self and to God. The resolution is that we use our time well; for we can renew body, mind, and soul, but time cannot be renewed. Each day of this retreat counts. The certainty—which each of us can test for himself or herself—is that the first day of retreat has brought us a small measure of God's peace, and a connection to the great tradition in which we work.

As night closes in, I suggest that each of us spend a few minutes going over the events of the day, measuring its ups and downs. Don't hesitate to record in your journal any insights that have come your way; you will be grateful later for the record that you keep now.

Let us end the day by reflecting on the following paean to prayer—an astonishing cascade of images culminating in two unforgettable last words—by the country parson and metaphysical poet George Herbert (1593–1633). In it, you will find all the themes of the day, and more. I suggest that you read the poetry sprinkled throughout this book just as you read the Divine Office: aloud, enunciating each word, listening with all the attention you can muster to the poem's symphony of sound and meaning.

Prayer, the Church's banquet, Angels' age,
    God's breath in man returning to his birth,
The soul in paraphrase, heart in pilgrimage,
    The Christian plummet, sounding heaven and earth;
Engine against the Almighty, sinner's tower,
    Reversed thunder, Christ-side-piercing spear,
The six-days' world transposing in an hour,
    A kind of tune, which all things hear and fear;
Softness, and peace, and joy, and love, and bliss,
    Exalted manna, gladness of the best,
    Heaven in ordinary, man well drest,
The milky way, the bird of Paradise,
    Church-bells beyond the stars heard, the soul's blood,
    The land of spices; something understood.

Chapter Five

DAY TWO

THE PATTERN FOR TODAY

Today—Saturday —marks the middle of our sojourn. In the miniature life of this retreat, we are no longer babes and not yet elders; we can look both forward and back. This middle position gives us special privileges and responsibilities. Today we will receive unexpected insights, but we will also be tested in ways we can't foresee. We may be tempted to take it easy—or to bear down on ourselves. Let us instead decide at the outset to maintain a steady course, keeping in mind yesterday's promise of stability, which remains valid today. We have taken on what the Bible calls the yoke (in Sanskrit, *yoga*) of Christ, fashioned from love. Let us rejoice, for this yoga will set us free:

> Come to me, all you that are weary and are carrying heavy burdens, and I will give you rest. Take my yoke upon you, and learn from me; for I am gentle and humble in heart, and you will find rest for your souls. For my yoke is easy, and my burden is light.
>
> *(Matthew 11:28–30)*

As on Friday, we begin the day with thirty minutes of contemplative prayer (if necessary, refer to the instructions in chapter 4).

Once again, the monastic occupations of the Divine Office, *lectio divina,* and manual labor lend stability, balance, and rhythm to our waking hours. The text for sacred reading remains up to you. You might consider the following passage—one of the most profound in the entire New Testament—which has much to say about today's theme of spiritual gestation: the "high priestly prayer" of Jesus: John 17:1–25.

As for manual labor, a question surfaces: Should we continue with Friday's work or begin a new enterprise? Sustaining a task that we began yesterday will allow us to refine our skills, erase any errors that have crept in, and perhaps even see the job through to completion. On the other hand, we should drop any activity that has grown stale or habitual, for we run the risk of working in a distracted, haphazard way, rather than with the awakened attention that we seek.

For the Divine Office, too, we retain yesterday's approach. By now you should be well versed in chanting the psalms. If formerly you recited them silently out of timidity or bashfulness, today you can speak them aloud, as intended. Saturday's selections appear below. Notice that in order to save space, only new material—psalms and readings that vary day by day, known collectively as the "proper"—has been supplied. For material that never varies—canticles, opening and closing prayers, the Lord's Prayer, the Salve Regina, and so on, known as the "ordinary"—only the headings have been supplied. If necessary, refresh your memory by referring to chapter 4.

Lauds

INTRODUCTORY PRAYER

MORNING PSALM (PSALM 119:145–52)

> With my whole heart I cry; answer me, O Lord.
> I will keep your statutes.
> I cry to you; save me,

that I may observe your decrees.
I rise before dawn and cry for help;
    I put my hope in your words.
My eyes are awake before each watch of the night,
    that I may meditate on your promise.
In your steadfast love hear my voice;
    O Lord, in your justice preserve my life.
Those who persecute me with evil purpose draw
        near;
    they are far from your law.
Yet you are near, O Lord,
    and all your commandments are true.
Long ago I learned from your decrees
    that you have established them forever.

(Bow) Glory be . . .

OLD TESTAMENT CANTICLE (EZEKIEL 36:26–28)

A new heart I will give you, and a new spirit I will put
within you; and I will remove from your body the heart of
stone and give you a heart of flesh. I will put my spirit
within you, and make you follow my statutes and be careful to observe my ordinances. Then you shall live in the
land that I gave to your ancestors, and you shall be my
people, and I will be your God.

(Bow) Glory be . . .

PSALM OF PRAISE (PSALM 8)

O Lord, our Sovereign,
    how majestic is your name in all the earth!

You have set your glory above the heavens.
    Out of the mouths of babes and infants
you have founded a bulwark because of your foes,
    to silence the enemy and the avenger.

When I look at your heavens, the work of your
    fingers,
    the moon and the stars that you have established;
what are human beings that you are mindful of
    them,
    mortals that you care for them?

Yet you have made them a little lower than God,
    and crowned them with glory and honor.
You have given them dominion over the works of
    your hands;
    you have put all things under their feet,
all sheep and oxen,
    and also the beasts of the field,
the birds of the air, and the fish of the sea,
    whatever passes along the paths of the seas.

O Lord, our Sovereign,
    how majestic is your name in all the earth!

(Bow) Glory be . . .

SCRIPTURE READING (ROMANS 12:14–16A)

Bless those who persecute you; bless and do not curse
them. Rejoice with those who rejoice, weep with those
who weep. Live in harmony with one another.

SILENT PRAYER

GOSPEL CANTICLE OF ZECHARIAH

THE LORD'S PRAYER

CONCLUDING PRAYER

BLESSING

The Recollected Heart

INTRODUCTORY PRAYER

PSALM (PSALM 113)

Praise the Lord!
Praise, O servants of the Lord;
     praise the name of the Lord.

Blessed be the name of the Lord
     from this time on and forevermore.
From the rising of the sun to its setting
     the name of the Lord is to be praised.
The Lord is high above all nations,
     and his glory above the heavens.

Who is like the Lord our God,
     who is seated on high,
who looks far down
     on the heavens and the earth?
He raises the poor from the dust,
     and lifts the needy from the ash heap,
to make them sit with princes,
     with the princes of his people.
He gives the barren woman a home,
     making her the joyous mother of children.
Praise the Lord!

(Bow) Glory be . . .

PSALM (PSALM 16)

Protect me, O God, for in you I take refuge.
I say to the Lord, "You are my Lord;
     I have no good apart from you."

As for the holy ones in the land, they are the noble,
     in whom is all my delight.

Those who choose another god multiply their
    sorrows;
    their drink offerings of blood I will not pour out
    or take their names upon my lips.

The Lord is my chosen portion and my cup;
    you hold my lot.
The boundary lines have fallen for me in pleasant
    places;
    I have a goodly heritage.

I bless the Lord who gives me counsel;
    in the night also my heart instructs me.
I keep the Lord always before me;
    because he is at my right hand, I shall not be
        moved.

Therefore my heart is glad, and my soul rejoices;
    for my body also rests secure.
For you do not give me up to Sheol,
    or let your faithful one see the Pit.

You show me the path of life.
    In your presence there is fullness of joy;
    in your right hand are pleasures forevermore.

(Bow) Glory be . . .

NEW TESTAMENT CANTICLE (PHILIPPIANS 2:5–9)

Let the same mind be in you that was in Christ Jesus,
who, though he was in the form of God,
    did not regard equality with God
    as something to be exploited,
but emptied himself,
    taking the form of a slave,

being born in human likeness.
And being found in human form,
  he humbled himself
  and become obedient to the point of death—
  even death on a cross.

Therefore God also highly exalted him
  and gave him the name
  that is above every name.

(Bow) Glory be . . .

SCRIPTURE READING (ROMANS 8:35, 37–39)

Who will separate us from the love of Christ? Will hardship, or distress, or persecution, or famine, or nakedness, or peril, or sword? No, in all these things we are more than conquerors through him who loved us. For I am convinced that neither death, nor life, nor angels, nor rulers, nor things present, nor things to come, nor powers, nor height, nor depth, nor anything else in all creation, will be able to separate us from the love of God in Christ Jesus our Lord.

SILENT PRAYER

GOSPEL CANTICLE OF MARY

THE LORD'S PRAYER

CONCLUDING PRAYER

BLESSING

Compline

INTRODUCTORY PRAYER

EXAMINATION OF CONSCIENCE

PSALM (PSALM 134)

> Come bless the Lord, all you servants of the Lord,
>> who stand by night in the house of the Lord!
> Lift up your hands to the holy place,
>> and bless the Lord.
>
> May the Lord, maker of heaven and earth,
>> bless you from Zion.

(Bow) Glory be . . .

SCRIPTURE READING (DEUTERONOMY 6:4–7)

> Hear, O Israel: the Lord is our God, the Lord alone. You shall love the Lord your God with all your heart, and with all your soul, and with all your might. Keep these words that I am commanding you today in your heart. Recite them to your children and talk about them when you are at home and when you are away, when you lie down and when you rise.

SILENT PRAYER

GOSPEL CANTICLE

CONCLUDING PRAYER

BLESSING

SALVE REGINA

Today's theme: Gestation

I once witnessed a tooth-and-nail debate between two friends, both advanced in spiritual understanding, over the nature of enlightenment. Mr. A, a poet much influenced by Zen, argued for instantaneous awakening: Liberation, he felt, could come in a flash at any moment. Ms. B, a philosopher, vehemently disagreed: Spiritual truth, she said, sat atop a mountain that took a lifetime to climb. I enjoyed the debate, for there's nothing more revealing than to see two people whom one admires lose their sangfroid in the pitch of mental strife. Truth, I reminded myself, is as slippery as a snake, and at one time or another, everyone loses his grip. However, after a few hours of give-and-take, Mr. A and Ms. B reached a consensus. Let us suppose, they said, that truth straddles both positions. Could it be that instant enlightenment is a chimera, that behind it lie years of preparation? And could it be, conversely, that all inner illumination, however slow the prelude, includes a sudden influx or quantum burst of light?

As this anecdote reveals, today's theme of spiritual gestation turns out—like all real subjects—to be richer than we usually acknowledge. Much about it remains mysterious, from its duration to its form. Just to complicate things a bit more (with an eye toward clarity down the road), let us take a brief hike into the boggy moors of Latin and English grammar. The English verb "to gestate" derives from the Latin *gerare,* "to carry." In the time of Shakespeare, people might say "the mother gestates the baby" (just as we still say "the mother carries the baby"). Over time, however, a significant linguistic transformation took place, and we now speak of the baby gestating in the womb. The role of the baby has become active rather than passive.

At first glance, this observation might seem far removed from our subject, but in fact it tells us a great deal about the monastic meaning of gestation. For from the monastic vantage point, each of us is an unborn child mothered by God, who bears us, gestates us, and brings us to new birth. At the same time, we carry ourselves toward delivery; we remain responsible for our own self-development. The work is mutual, and both senses of gestation—the ancient and the new—obtain. We gestate ourselves and God gestates us. Or, to use a related idiom, we must learn to be both children and adults in relation to God. We need the maturity to become innocents again. Realizing our nature as God's children (and the adult responsibility that this entails) lies at the heart of Jesus' teaching: "Truly I tell you, unless you change and become like children, you will never enter the kingdom of heaven" (Matthew 18:3). Paul explains how this is to be done:

> For once you were darkness, but now in the Lord you are light. Live as children of light—for the fruit of the light is found in all that is good and right and true. Try to find out what is pleasing to the Lord. *(Ephesians 5:8–10)*

Adoption as God's children comes though an ardent search for the "good and right and true," an extended gestation in the womb of spiritual discernment. During this process, we must not rely exclusively on ourselves (for in the end our very existence depends on God), nor must we abjure personal responsibility and idly await our transformation (for a prize won without struggle is no prize at all). Once again, the Benedictine principle of balance applies.

Here is an exercise to help us appreciate the nuances of gestation, the slow, introspective growth that characterizes all creation:

Remembering Our Ancestors

Our inner gestation didn't begin yesterday, when we shut the door against the outside world and commenced our retreat. Whatever wisdom we discover this weekend rests on a foundation laid brick-by-brick during all the years of our life. Nor did gestation start here; in most cases, our parents prepared the ground for our spiritual formation. And even this description falls short, for our parents' work depended on that of their parents, and so on and so on, back across the vast sweep of generations that flickered into and out of existence over millions of years, until we arrive at the seed itself, in the crude ruttings of Pleistocene protohumans or the chaste loins of Adam and Eve.

Only the tip of this great transgenerational cord of life remains available to us, and even that grows more truncated every year. Not so long ago, people could identify their ancestors back five or six generations. Now, few of us can name our great-grandparents. What a terrible loss this collective amnesia is, for family history not only gives us definition, but it makes us aware of the tremendous debt we owe our forebears. A million fathers and mothers preceded each of us, a million gestations about which we know nothing. In a sense, we are the product of a single, great gestation spanning unimaginable epochs, unknown cultures, unnamed ancestors beyond reckoning.

In the face of this boundless generosity, we naturally turn to yesterday's prayer theme of thanksgiving. I would like to suggest, as an appropriate way to begin, that you spend a few minutes writing down the names of your ancestors, as far back as possible. Your parents or adoptive parents will do, if that marks the limit of recall. Consider in turn each name on the list. Let's pick, as an example, your great-grandfather Antony. If you knew Antony during his lifetime, if he dandled you on his knee or taught you how to drive, bring him to mind as vividly as you can. Remember his voice, his walk, the way he laughed, shook hands, cradled a coffee cup. Resurrect him in your memory. Once he stands before you, give him thanks for transmitting life to you. Try to find yourself in him, and he in you. Without this man, you would be nothing.

If the name before you is that of a collateral ancestor (cousin, aunt, uncle), it makes no difference. He or she deserves gratitude all the same; for every ancestor, however remote, shared in the building of the family whose flesh gave birth to you. Nor does it matter if the ancestor died long before your birth: Here imagination supplants memory, while the task remains the same—to thank those who came before you for the gift of life. You may, if you wish, extend your thanks by praying to God for the welfare of the deceased.

Today's Promise: Obedience

My sixth-grade teacher, whom I will call Mr. Barnstable, a man with a remarkable moustache that flared out like rapiers on either side of his face, announced one day that he was dividing our class into two groups for the study of mathematics. One group would consist of advanced pupils; everyone else would be clumped into the "normal" group. To my dismay, Mr. Barnstable plunked me with the normals. For weeks I seethed at this injustice, for I was a lightning-fast calculator and believed that I belonged with the elite. Finally, I spoke up. My teacher smiled broadly—a vaguely threatening gesture, as it set his hairy swords abristle—and promised to promote me if I would solve a little problem that, he assured me, "anyone in the advanced group could lick in a minute." To this day I recall the puzzle, for it is burned into a special corner of my brain reserved for painful memories: He asked me to divide 238 by 17. I had never run across long division before. Instantly, my hopes shattered against the invincible wall of ignorance. Mr. Barnstable looked at me, and I read pity in his eyes. This was the final blow. I dissolved into tears and ran from the room.

For months afterward, I nursed my injured pride. Years passed before I settled down enough to discern the problem behind the problem. To put it simply, I had failed to learn math in the proper sequence. I had tried to jump over some necessary steps, to disrupt the normal gestation of my mathematical mind. There are laws to mathematics, as to everything else, and I had flouted those laws.

This, I believe, is the real meaning of obedience, the second promise made by Benedictine monks and nuns upon entering the monastery. Benedictines pledge to discover the principles and procedures (that is to say, the laws) of the spiritual life, and to follow them unswervingly. Obedience derives from the Latin root *oboedire,* "to listen to." One who obeys is one who listens. (This idea also appears in Hebrew, which has no single word for "obey"; the act is conveyed by two other verbs: "to listen" and "to do.") The monk listens above all to the abbot and surrenders to his will. In this transaction, however, the abbot "is believed to hold the place of Christ in the monastery," as Benedict writes in the *Rule* (RB 2). In effect, then, the monk places himself eagerly, continually, and utterly under God's will, by following "the superior's order as promptly as if the command came from God himself." God, abbot, and monk sound a single chord—one initiated by God—that brings harmony to all who join in. In the first and final stanzas of the *Paradiso,* at the inception and culmination of his long, perilous ascent to truth, Dante Alighieri describes this state of holy obedience at its most exalted, and the conditions that inspire it:

> The glory of the One Who moves all things
>   penetrates the universe and shines
>   in one part more and in another less . . .
>
> Here power failed the highest fantasy;
>   but already my desire and will,
>   like the wheel spinning in perfect balance,
>   were being turned
> By the Love that moves the sun and the other stars.

From Dante's verse, an exquisite truth emerges. Love powers all: the Sun across the sky, the stars in their yearly course, the turning wheel. What science calls the law of physics, Christian tradition sees as the law of God, synonymous with love. All things revolve in love and thus in obedience around the Maker of all things. Our own inner life is no exception. We orbit God by following the laws of the spiritual life, guidelines to our own good and that of others. An aboriginal proverb from Australia puts it succinctly: "Human beings are made for the Law, not the Law for human beings." Law, as Chesterton observes in *The Man Who Was Thursday,* is the track that guides the train to its destination. Listen to his poet-policeman declaim with typical Chestertonian paradox upon the theme:

> The rare, strange thing is to hit the mark; the gross, obvious thing is to miss it. We feel it is epical when man with one wild arrow strikes a distant bird. Is it not also epical when man with one wild engine strikes a distant station? Chaos is dull, because in chaos the train might indeed go anywhere, to Baker Street or to Bagdad. But man is a magician, and his whole magic is in this, that he does say Victoria, and lo! it is Victoria. No, take your books of mere poetry and prose; let me read a time table, with tears of pride. . . . every time a train comes in I feel that it has broken past batteries of besiegers, and that man has won a battle against chaos.

May all our trains run on time—but assuredly, they won't. We will enjoy many opportunities to struggle with obedience, as our train threatens to derail for a number of reasons, including sloth, despair, and self-love. Today's course offers more than its share of bumps. Be certain of this: Difficulties will seek us out. As Martin Luther aptly put it, "a thousand devils hurl themselves against me in my solitude." Once the initial thrill of retreat wears off, we may begin to feel homesick or bored or depressed by our isolation. Now, obedience becomes a real concern. Do we confront our difficulties or turn away? Stay put or escape?

Many of us will wrestle with contemplative prayer. After five or ten minutes, we may feel a desperate need to stand up, run around, wave our arms, shout hello. We may, by way of contrast, find ourselves growing groggy during the prayer or even nodding off. If such physical difficulties strike, my advice is to *stick with it*. Without a dash of fortitude, we can get nowhere. Many people complain about distraction during contemplation: They plunge into fantastic daydreams, they visit India or Tibet while sitting on their cushions. The only answer is to *stick with it*. Gently return to the task at hand, to the cushion, to the heart, to God.

Perhaps you find yourself overwhelmed by fear, or loneliness or self-pity or bitterness wells up and threatens to drown you. Again, the best advice is, *stick with it*. In these crises we hear the death rattle of the ego, a creature who can take a lifetime to die. Be patient. Often a spell of reading helps. Or change your activity—go for a walk, cook, listen to music. Write down your feelings and thoughts; this may release some of the pent-up poison.

In the final analysis, all these problems become one problem, that of obedience. If we obey our hearts and forge ahead, we will learn to welcome stumbling blocks as splendid opportunities for self-knowledge and self-overcoming (as did Sam when the paint rained down). Some of our best insights come when the world goes haywire, when the chicken turns black in the oven and marsh water soaks the sleeping bag, when we find ourselves frustrated in prayer and foolish in action. For then we see who we really are, and we see in Whom our real hope lies. This marks the beginning of real retreat, real perspective, real prayer. In contemplation, these obstacles may culminate in a period of spiritual aridity. God seems absent. Prayer loses its savor. The seeker feels lost, abandoned, bereft of hope. But in truth, this time of trial—which John of the Cross named "the dark night of the soul"—may prove to be God's greatest gift, an initiation into spiritual maturity, the birth pangs of the new human being. Take refuge in the Lord, as the Psalmist advises, for "the Lord is my rock, my fortress, and my deliverer" (Psalm 18:2). Trust in God, and be at peace.

At the same time, obedience means knowing what works and what doesn't. An intelligent runner won't push his leg muscles beyond the tearing point. How much more true of us, as we run toward God. I choose this metaphor deliberately, for the Bible teems with images of sprinting: "Those who wait for the Lord . . . shall run and not be weary" (Isaiah 40:31); "Let us run with perseverance the race that is set before us" (Hebrews 12:1). On the second day of our retreat, we find ourselves in the middle of the marathon. This means that we respect our limits (which is why we withdraw from the world for three days rather than for three years). It also means that, like any athlete, we search out the right conditions for our efforts. In the following passage, Jacques Lusseyran describes the importance to his inner world of a deserted storeroom:

> You can imagine what a big empty room would mean to a blind child. . . . I spent endless hours in the storeroom that summer. I was almost always alone there, but this solitude was densely populated with all kinds of shapes and with the inventions of a personage I had never known before: myself. . . . I was in the state that all children reach sooner or later when, thank heaven, there is no more past or future, no dream or reality, but only themselves riding on life at a gallop.[1]

In this room, Lusseyran discovers stability, freedom, life itself. He comes to this happy state through obedience by listening to the needs of his imagination and his blindness and finding the right conditions to join the two, so that imagination can heal blindness and blindness can set imagination free ("to listen to" and "to do," the twin components of "obey" in Hebrew, as we have seen).

Benedictine monasticism employs a special image to describe this process of self-knowledge through obedience: the ladder of humility. This is a most peculiar ladder, built of the wood of paradox, for on it one descends in order to ascend; as the monk or nun clambers down into greater humility—that is, toward final escape from the selfish ego and its chains—the higher he or she goes toward God. By humility, as I said in chapter 2, Benedict doesn't mean humiliation (which violates the dignity of all human beings), but rather humbleness, a state of being, akin to that of contemplative prayer, in which we await the refining fire of God's love. Our surest means of ascent comes by way of the Beatitudes, which counsel mercy over vengeance, meekness over self-assertion, peace over rancor. "Let us love one another," writes the anonymous author of 2 John, who hastens to explain that "this is love, that we walk according to his commandments," thus making explicit the marriage of obedience, humility, and goodness that leads to wisdom. Benedict asks his monks to greet all visitors with a bow; we needn't carry our practice this far—although it would do no harm—but certainly we should make every effort to discern Christ's presence in everyone we meet.

A second approach to the ladder of humility comes through self-denial. With this in mind, I would like to suggest an experiment in asceticism. I imagine that at the mere mention of this word, you may have fainted dead away. No need to fear. We'll keep the hair shirts and whips in mothballs for another day. Instead, I propose a simple discipline native to almost all religious traditions: a small fast. This abstinence from overeating (almost all of us eat too much) can take two forms:

1. Consume only half of your ordinary allotment of food at breakfast, lunch, and dinner.
2. Give up eating between meals.

For most of us, accustomed to munching on cookies or carrots whenever we please, the latter program may prove to be the more arduous of the two. Whichever you choose, I suggest that whenever you feel a pang of hunger, you use it as today's "sign," a summons to recollection, an invitation to prayer. Obviously, this modest fast won't bring you into a state of altered consciousness. Rigorous purging through intensive abstinence from food can be immensely useful, but it exhausts the body and would be counterproductive on this retreat. Save it for another time. Rest assured, however, that even a gentle fast will sharpen your attention, lighten your body, and sweeten your mind. In addition, fasting leads to humbleness, as we see our utter dependence on such lowly things as water and grain, which reflect our true dependence on the highest of all Beings.

PETITIONARY PRAYER

As we struggle with obstacles, distractions, fears—the intimidating line up we face every day—sooner or later we will feel overwhelmed. No matter how diligently we clear the trail, the brambles surge back. We will never be free of tribulation. For just this reason, we need petitionary prayer.

In this form of prayer, perhaps the most basic of all, we appeal to God for help. God answers our prayers, as Jesus pledged ("Knock, and the door will be opened for you,"

Matthew 7:7) and as millions of people can attest.[2] However, God responds to our needs, not to our fantasies. Pray for a cherry-red sports car, and God may answer your prayer by granting you the wisdom to make a more mature request. Pray for tranquility, and you will receive your share. Nothing could be more certain, for you will soon discover that petitionary prayer itself brings peace, that it stills the body, soothes the heart, settles the mind, and draws us to God. Prayers uttered on the verge of life and death—prayers of a soldier in battle, of a mother in childbirth—rush us to God, in whose arms we may begin to glimpse the spiritual meaning of suffering. God hears our distress, whether we know it or not. In ways that we may be too distraught or too blind to discern, God listens and responds.

But why do we need to pray? Doesn't God know our desires before we give them voice? How can it be that the One who "laid the foundation of the earth" (Job 38:4) is swayed by our tiny voices? Many theologians have tried to unravel this knot. The best explanation I have heard comes from Jean-Marie Cardinal Lustiger, Archbishop of Paris: God's relationship to each of us is analogous to that of parent to child (as we have already discussed). Now, as many of us can confirm from personal experience, we often know our children's desires before they ask, but we like to be asked nonetheless. We wish this, says Lustiger, not because it preens our egos, but because it deepens the exchange of love between parent and child.

In just the same way, we ask God for help as we struggle toward spiritual rebirth. While I imagine none of us is so immature as to request a winning lottery ticket, we needn't restrict our prayers to abstractions like peace or love. God, the Supreme Artist, abhors generalities as much as any human creator. When Van Gogh dreamt of peace, he painted a field of Provençal wheat drenched in sunlight. In the same way, when we ask for serenity, we do well to translate our wish into specifics. Pray for what will bring you real peace: the courage to control your anger toward your brother, or the good health to begin a new job. Be sure to pray to your saint, to help you pray to God. Around the world, people in dire straits still petition St. Jude, patron of hopeless causes (no one knows how poor Jude received this onerous job, although the similarity of his name to that of Judas Iscariot suggests a case of mistaken identity). Often such a prayer will be as simple as "Dear St. Jude, fly to my assistance. Ask God to help me with this special need." Such a pure prayer is certain to reach God's ears.

TODAY'S PRAYER PRACTICE: THE JESUS PRAYER

One late autumn day in the mid–nineteenth century, a thirty-three-year-old man with a withered arm set out on pilgrimage across czarist Russia in search of the secrets of perfect prayer. He carried only some dry husks of bread, a Bible, and an invincible longing for God. At first, his mission seemed fruitless. Begging for instruction, he received only lofty sermons from priests and laypeople alike. But the pilgrim hungered for more than abstractions; he sought a sure method to bring him to God. Eventually he met a *staretz*—a church elder—who supplied the key in the form of the "Jesus Prayer." This prayer, methodically recited day in and day out, changed the pilgrim's life:

> Sometimes my heart would feel as though it were bubbling with joy; such lightness, freedom, and consolation were in it. Sometimes I felt a burning love for Jesus Christ and for all God's creatures. Sometimes my eyes brimmed over with tears of thankfulness to God, who was so merciful to me, a wretched sinner. . . . Sometimes by calling upon the name of Jesus I was overwhelmed with bliss, and now I knew the meaning of the words, "The Kingdom of God is within you."[3]

The pilgrim wandered the land for several years, continuing to practice the Jesus Prayer. Every encounter became a lesson in grace. A wolf attacked him but succumbed to his holiness and ran away. He was flogged, exiled, frozen from a fall into icy waters. Through these trials, he slowly changed from seeker to teacher, sufferer to healer. The Jesus Prayer, he told all who would listen, brought to its practitioners

> understanding of Holy Scripture, knowledge of the speech of created things, freedom from fuss and vanity, knowledge of the joy of the inner life, and finally certainty of the nearness of God and of His love for us.[4]

Nearly a century and a half later, the story of this anonymous Russian pilgrim continues to fascinate (most recently in the 1960s, when J. D. Salinger—fittingly, a recluse on permanent retreat from the New York literary scene— made the Jesus Prayer the centerpiece of his best-selling novella, *Franny and Zooey*). Yet the sustained life of the prayer depends not on cultural trends but on the simplicity and integrity of its form. In its most basic form, one merely says "Lord Jesus Christ, have mercy on me." In the monasteries of Mt. Athos, Greece's holy mountain, the formula has expanded at times into the more cumbersome "Lord Jesus Christ, Son and Word of the living God, through the prayers of thy most pure Mother and of all the Saints, have mercy on us and save us."

The Jesus Prayer is petitionary prayer at its purest; in effect, it is Christianity compressed to seven words. We ask for mercy from God, in the person of Jesus Christ. By so doing, we acknowledge our faith in God's power, compassion and love. Some Orthodox saints of the hesychast school (*hesychia* is Greek for "tranquility") believe that the prayer bestows on its practitioners the "divine energies," a technical term that we may loosely define as God's manifest presence. When we pray the Jesus Prayer, it is said, God prays with us; heaven and earth unite in holy invocation. According to tradition, the prayer derives its power from the numinous power of God's name, revealed to Moses during his Sinai retreat; its form from the passage in Luke (18:35–43) in which a blind man from Jericho shouts out "Jesus, Son of David, have mercy on me!" and regains his sight; its prestige from Jesus' promise that "if you ask anything of the Father in my name, he will give it to you" (John 16:23).

The Jesus Prayer should be said slowly and distinctly, heeding the meaning of each word, just as we recite the Divine Office. Repeat the prayer often; the pilgrim reports saying it a staggering 6,000 times a day! To keep track, many people use a prayer rope, the simple woolen string divided into 50 or 100 knots, described in detail in chapter 3. In some Orthodox monasteries, each repetition is accompanied by a deep bow or even a full prostration, forehead to floor. Perhaps it would be best to avoid such exertions during our brief retreat. However, I encourage you to say the prayer in all circumstances: walking in the woods, driving, sewing, rocking a baby. You may pray out loud, or subvocalize the words, or keep the mouth still and sound the words in your heart.

Observance of the Jesus Prayer may continue for a lifetime. Eventually, you may notice certain changes in your practice. The pilgrim reports, and other practitioners confirm, that after a while the prayer becomes self-acting, moving from the conscious to the subconscious mind, then from the mind into the heart, until finally one recites it at all times, whether eating or talking or taking a bath, alert or drowsy, awake or asleep. More commonly, however, one's practice of the prayer flags for a while and then revitalizes when the need is felt again.

FINISHING THE DAY

I recommend that we complete the second day of our retreat just as we did the first, with contemplative prayer, Compline, and quiet recreation. As a fitting conclusion to the day, I propose an experiment in self-examination. Begin by making a list of your "enemies," those people whom you dislike or avoid or even hate. You needn't come up with someone who sends you into cardiac arrest; think of a person whose face you find unpleasant or whose political beliefs you reject. Remember now how the Dalai Lama treated China. Each of these people is your "China": an apparent enemy who may be transformed, through humility and with God's help, into a genuine friend.

Dwell on each person in turn. Picture this woman—an old business associate who talks when she should listen and never follows your advice—as she eats dinner, tucks her children into bed, takes Rover for a romp. Does her image arouse in you pity, anger, envy? All these feelings play a part in our dislike of another. If, by magic, you suddenly switched lives with her, how would you react? Can you see the justice of her ways? How do you suppose she looks at you? What now of your judgments, your condemnations?

Carry this exercise one step further. Death, the great leveler, is the great leavener as well. In the face of death—even an exercise in imaginary death— we may rise to new heights of love and understanding. Monks and nuns value reminders of death: thus the black of the Benedictine habit, or the tombstone-shaped hats of Islamic dervishes, or the ancient ascetic practice (found in Christianity, Buddhism, and other religions) of picturing the decay of one's corpse. Imagine each of your so-called enemies—who are, in truth, your secret friends—on the brink of death, calling out to you for help. How will you respond? What resources of love do their cries summon in you?

As the day draws to a close, you might wish to record in your journal any insights or impressions that seem important. Avoid making judgments: A clear, concise record of the day will serve you best, now and later.

Let us end Saturday by meditating on two petitionary prayer-poems. The first is a hymn from medieval England; the second, a prayer by novelist Jane Austen (1775–1817). Again, I advise you to read each poem aloud, slowly and reflectively.

HYMN

> God be in my hede
>   And in my understandyng,
> God be in myne eyes
>   And in my loking,
> God be in my mouth
>   And in my speaking,
> God be in my harte
>   And in my thynkyng,
> God be in mine ende
>   And at my departyng.
> —*Anonymous*

PRAYER

> Incline us O God! to think humbly of ourselves, to be saved only in the examination of our own conduct, to consider our fellow-creatures with kindness, and to judge of all they say and do with the charity which we would desire from them ourselves.
>
> —*Jane Austen*

Chapter Six

DAY THREE

The Pattern for Today

Sunday, the day of resurrection and rebirth, marks the coming-of-age of our retreat. The fertilizing, planting, and pruning end; today, the tree bears fruit. Let us be sure to take the time to gather a full harvest. Perhaps we're already looking ahead to tonight or tomorrow, when we will return to ordinary life. Or perhaps we're casting a jaundiced eye over the last two days, wishing we could have them back to do over again. Future and past tug at our sleeves. I suggest that we respond with an extraordinary attempt at recollection, mustering all the attention we can, making a special effort in all our prayers, labors, and exercises. Let us, as Thoreau advised, "live deeply and suck out all the marrow."

We begin, as always, with thirty minutes of contemplation. Today I'd like us to pay particular attention to our state immediately after leaving the prayer. What is this tranquility that we feel in bone and blood as well as in the mind? What sustains it? What steals it away? Perhaps we can learn a little more about the nature of contemplative prayer, and how to integrate it into our ordinary lives, by seeing how its qualities evaporate when we rise from our sitting cushions.

Once again, the Divine Office marks the phases of the day. The texts can be found below (as usual, only the proper is supplied; for the ordinary, see chapter 4). I suggest that for *lectio divina* you continue to read whatever material you began on Friday, or else turn to the following passage, which has much to say about today's theme of resurrection: the parable of the prodigal son, Luke 15:11–32

As for manual labor, you can either finish yesterday's work or begin something new. But bear in mind that our retreat ends this evening; this isn't the time to start a long-range project.

The Divine Office for Sunday is as follows:

Lauds

INTRODUCTORY PRAYER

MORNING PSALM (PSALM 63:1–8)

O God, you are my God, I seek you,
  my soul thirsts for you;
my flesh faints for you,
  as in a dry and weary land where there is no water.
So I have looked upon you in the sanctuary,
  beholding your power and glory.
Because your steadfast love is better than life,
  my lips will praise you.
So I will bless you as long as I live;
  I will lift up my hands and call on your name.

My soul is satisfied as with a rich feast,
  and my mouth praises you with joyful lips
when I think of you on my bed,

and meditate on you in the watches of the night;
for you have been my help,
    and in the shadow of your wings I sing for joy.
My soul clings to you;
    your right hand upholds me.

(Bow) Glory be . . .

OLD TESTAMENT CANTICLE (DANIEL 3:52–57; ALSO
KNOWN AS THE PRAYER OF AZARIAH, 29–34)

Blessed are you, O Lord, God of our ancestors,
    and to be praised and highly exalted forever;
And blessed is your glorious, holy name,
    and to be highly praised and highly exalted
      forever.
Blessed are you in the temple of your holy glory,
    and to be extolled and highly glorified forever.
Blessed are you who look into the depths from your
      throne on the cherubim,
    and to be praised and highly exalted forever.
Blessed are you on the throne of your kingdom,
    and to be extolled and highly exalted forever.
Blessed are you in the firmament of heaven,
    and to be sung and glorified forever.

(Bow) Glory be . . .

PSALM OF PRAISE (PSALM 148)

Praise the Lord!
Praise the Lord from the heavens;
    praise him in the heights!
Praise him, all his angels,
    praise him, all his host!

Praise him, sun and moon;
  praise him, all you shining stars!
Praise him, you highest heavens,
  and you waters above the heavens!

Let them praise the name of the Lord,
  for he commanded and they were created.
He established them forever and ever;
  he fixed their bounds, which cannot be passed.

Praise the Lord from the earth,
  you sea monsters and all deeps,
fire and hail, snow and frost,
  stormy wind fulfilling his command!

Mountains and all hills,
  fruit trees and all cedars!
Wild animals and all cattle,
  creeping things and flying birds!

Kings of the earth and all peoples,
  princes and all rulers of the earth!
Young men and women alike,
  old and young together!
Let them praise the name of the Lord,
  for his name alone is exalted;
  his glory is above earth and heaven.
He has raised up a horn for his people,
  praise for all his faithful,
  for the people of Israel who are close to him.
Praise the Lord!

(Bow) Glory be . . .

Thus says the Lord God: I am going to open your graves, and bring you up from your graves, O my people; and I will bring you back to the land of Israel. And you shall know that I am the Lord, when I open your graves, and bring you up from your graves, O my people. I will put my spirit within you, and you shall live, and I will place you on your own soil; then you shall know that I, the Lord, have spoken and will act.

SILENT PRAYER

GOSPEL CANTICLE OF ZECHARIAH

THE LORD'S PRAYER

CONCLUDING PRAYER

BLESSING

Vespers

INTRODUCTORY PRAYER

PSALM (PSALM 110:2–4)

> The Lord sends out from Zion
>> your mighty scepter.
>> Rule in the midst of your foes.
> Your people will offer themselves willingly
>> on the day you lead your forces
>> on the holy mountains.
> From the womb of the morning,
>> like dew, your youth will come to you.

(Bow) Glory be . . .

Praise the Lord!
I will give thanks to the Lord with my whole heart,
    in the company of the upright, in the
      congregation.
Great are the works of the Lord,
    studied by all who delight in them.
Full of honor and majesty is his work,
    and his righteousness endures forever.
He has gained renown by his wonderful deeds;
    the Lord is gracious and merciful.
He provides food for those who fear him;
    he is ever mindful of his covenant.
He has shown his people the power of his works,
    in giving them the heritage of the nations.
The work of his hands are faithful and just;
    all his precepts are trustworthy.
They are established forever and ever,
    to be performed with faithfulness and uprightness.
He sent redemption to his people;
    he has commanded his covenant forever.
    Holy and awesome is his name.
The fear of the Lord is the beginning of wisdom;
    all those who practice it have a good
      understanding.
    His praise endures forever.

(Bow) Glory be . . .

NEW TESTAMENT CANTICLE
(REVELATION 19:1–2, 5–7)

Hallelujah!
Salvation and glory and power to our God,

for his judgments are true and just.
Praise our God, all you his servants,
and all who fear him, small and great.
For the Lord our God the Almighty reigns.
Let us rejoice and exult and give him the glory.
For the marriage of the Lamb has come,
and his bride has made herself ready.

(Bow) Glory be . . .

SCRIPTURE READING (2 THESSALONIANS 2:13–14)

We must always give thanks to God for you, brothers and
sisters beloved by the Lord, because God chose you as the
first fruits for salvation through sanctification by the Spirit
and through belief in the truth. For this purpose he called
you through our proclamation of the good news, so that
you may obtain the glory of our Lord Jesus Christ.

SILENT PRAYER

GOSPEL CANTICLE OF MARY

THE LORD'S PRAYER

CONCLUDING PRAYER

BLESSING

Compline

INTRODUCTORY PRAYER

EXAMINATION OF CONSCIENCE

PSALM (PSALM 91)

You who live in the shelter of the Most High,
who abide in the shadow of the Almighty,

will say to the Lord, "My refuge and my fortress;
  my God, in whom I trust."
For he will deliver you from the snare of the fowler
  and from the deadly pestilence;
he will cover you with his pinions,
  and under his wings you will find refuge;
  his faithfulness is a shield and buckler.
You will not fear the terror of the night,
  or the arrow that flies by day,
or the pestilence that stalks in darkness,
  or the destruction that wastes at noonday.

A thousand may fall at your side,
  ten thousand at your right hand,
  but it will not come near you.
You will only look with your eyes
  and see the punishment of the wicked.

Because you have made the Lord your refuge,
  the Most High your dwelling place,
no evil shall befall you,
  no scourge come near your tent.

For he will command his angels concerning you
  to guard you in all your ways.
On their hands they will bear you up,
  so that you will not dash your foot against a stone.
You will tread on the lion and the adder,
  the young lion and the serpent you will trample
    under foot.

Those who love me, I will deliver;
  I will protect those who know my name.
When they call to me, I will answer them;
  I will be with them in trouble,

I will rescue them and honor them,
With long life I will satisfy them,
and show them my salvation.

(Bow) Glory be . . .

SCRIPTURE READING (REVELATION 22:3–5)

His servants will worship him; they will see his face, and
his name will be on their foreheads. And there will be no
more night; they need no light of lamp or sun, for the
Lord God will be their light, and they will reign forever
and ever.

SILENT PRAYER

GOSPEL CANTICLE

CONCLUDING PRAYER

BLESSING

SALVE REGINA

TODAY'S THEME: RESURRECTION

In 1933 a fisherman working the waters of the Indian Ocean
off the Comoro Islands hooked something utterly unexpected,
a stubby fish five feet long, with spherical scales, steel-blue
body, lobed tail, and vestigial lungs. The world was mesmer-
ized—but not only by the creature's implausible appearance,
which resembled more a beast from a Breughelian nightmare
than a genuine denizen of the deeps. More astonishing still
was the fish's identity, for a search through the ichthyo-
paleontological literature proved it to be a coelacanth, a species
that scientists believed to have perished some 350 million years

ago. This tale of a "living fossil" brought to the world the same shiver of wonder that we feel when a grizzled veteran blasts a game-winning home run or when the first crocuses break through their casket of snow: the astonishment of rebirth, of resurrection.

On every Sunday of the year, Christians celebrate the resurrection of Christ, the prototype of all resurrection and rebirth. St. Paul describes resurrection in these majestic terms:

> What is sown is perishable, what is raised is imperishable. It is sown in dishonor, it is raised in glory. It is sown in weakness, it is raised in power. It is sown a physical body, it is raised a spiritual body. *(1 Corinthians 15:42–44)*

As Paul indicates, resurrection means more than repetition, more than starting afresh: It means awakening to a new order of being. On our retreat, we too are invited to a foretaste of resurrection in this particular sense. On Friday, we made an effort to break the chains of the past. On Saturday, we nourished our resolve in the womb of silence, stillness, and peace. Now, on Sunday, we can begin to "walk in newness of life" as "children of God, and if children, then heirs" (Romans 6:4, 8:16–17), inheritors of God's greatest gift, this resurrection of being that lies at the center of the Christian life. In order to understand more of what this signifies, let us turn now to the last of the three Benedictine promises, that of *conversio*.

TODAY'S PROMISE: *CONVERSIO*

As I pointed out yesterday, when Greek Orthodox monks chant the Jesus Prayer, they sometimes accompany it with a full prostration, forehead touching the ground. The monks call this movement *metanoia,* a Greek term that means "change of mind." As one can see, "mind" here has a rather broad definition, for it includes within it the action of the body. Indeed, the heart participates as well, for prostration is a gesture of humility, a confession of our dependence on and love for God. Heart, body, mind: The entire human being participates in *"metanoia."* For this reason, the word is appropriately translated not simply as "change of mind," but, more richly, as "change of being."

Metanoia—or *conversio,* as Benedictines phrase it—is the third promise made by a monk or nun upon entering the monastery. We will make *conversio* the focus of Sunday's inner work. In truth, this striving toward God through self-transformation lies at the base of our entire retreat, and indeed of our entire spiritual life. The many concerns of Friday and Saturday—thanksgiving and petition, stability and obedience, the practice of the presence and the Jesus Prayer—all participate in the work of *conversio.* It underlies every aspect of monastic profession. Listen to this assessment by Thomas Merton, delivered to an assembly of Benedictine abbots in Thailand just a few hours before his death:

> When you stop and think a little bit about St. Benedict's concept of *conversatio morum,* that most mysterious of our vows, which is actually the most essential I believe, it can be interpreted as a commitment to total inner transformation of one sort or another—a commitment to become a completely new man. It seems to me that that could be regarded as the end of the monastic life, and that no matter where one attempts to do this, that remains the essential thing.[1]

The call to *conversio* rings throughout the New Testament. We encounter it first in the summons of John the Baptist, "Repent, for the kingdom of heaven is at hand" (Matthew 3:2). Repentance, which has accrued such negative connotations in modern usage, originally meant just this supreme transformation of being, from darkness to light, ignorance to knowledge, hate to love. Jesus often repeated John's words; his entire teaching can be summed up as a summons to *conversio,* in which the Beatitudes define both the qualities that initiate transformation and the blessings that ensue:

> Blessed are the poor in spirit, for theirs is the kingdom of heaven.
> Blessed are those who mourn, for they will be comforted.
> Blessed are the meek, for they will inherit the earth.
> Blessed are those who hunger and thirst for righteousness, for they will be filled.
> Blessed are the merciful, for they will receive mercy.
> Blessed are the pure in heart, for they will see God.
> Blessed are the peacemakers, for they will be called children of God.
> *(Matthew 5:3–9)*

To many people, *conversio* implies a sudden, breathtaking change in identity. An outstanding literary example of such a makeover occurs in Charles Dickens's *Christmas Carol;* when Ebenezer Scrooge awakens on December 25 after a night of visions, the first words to soar from his mouth are "I am not the man I was." In the deepest sense, he has followed Paul's counsel in Ephesians 4:22–24:

> to put away your former way of life, your old self, corrupt and deluded by its lusts, and to be renewed in the spirit of your minds, and to clothe yourselves with the new self, created according to the likeness of God in true righteousness and holiness.

Such inner earthquakes can change the outer world; witness the indelible effect of St. Francis's *conversio* on medieval Europe, or that of St. Augustine on the entire history of the West. However, radical transformations like these are rare, if not sui generis. Happily, God offers us another path to sanctity. In this we can rejoice, for few of us will ever undergo the sort of convulsive volte-face experienced by Scrooge. In any case, such explosive change only sets the stage. It can be compared to the titanic release of energy that hurls a rocket into space; once aloft, the real work begins, the long and arduous navigation to the stars. Far more germane to our own lives, I believe, is the humble, muted *conversio* that God calls us to undertake each day, each hour, each moment of our lives. This is the *conversio* of which St. Benedict writes. Here we must choose our guides with special care. Someone like St. Francis, who kissed lepers and communed with angels, may prove to be too extraordinary—too exalted—for our needs. Let us turn to someone more like ourselves, at least in outward circumstances: the well-fed, elegantly dressed, snugly housed, headstrong, somewhat spoiled girl who would become St. Thérèse of Lisieux, founder of the "little way."

What background can rival Thérèse's for coziness? She was the youngest of five daughters, born to a devout, well-to-do watchmaker and his doting wife, a family submerged in the plush silk-and-brocade comforts of late nineteenth-century French bourgeois life. Only one feature disturbs the banal composition of the scene: from an early age, Thérèse harbored an unshakable determination to "enter Carmel," the Order of Discalced Carmelites, the same religious society to which Brother Lawrence had belonged. To fulfill what she insisted was God's will for her, the girl concocted some audacious schemes, the most outrageous unfolding on a visit to Rome in 1887, when she breached the code of silence during an audience with Pope Leo XIII to whisper in the pontiff's ear, "Holy Father, in honor of your Jubilee, permit me to enter Carmel at the age of fifteen." Not surprisingly, the pope replied, "I don't understand very well." When the matter was explained, he sensibly assured Thérèse that "you will enter if God wills it."[2] And so God did, four months later.

This unexceptional girl, whose spunk puts us more in mind of Nancy Drew than someone of exalted sanctity, entered the Carmel at Lisieux, France, in 1888. She never again quit the monastery grounds; guests spoke to her through an iron grille (put in place, you will recall, not to keep the nuns in but to keep the world out). Eight years after her entrance, on Good Friday, 1896, Thérèse coughed up blood. The diagnosis was tuberculosis. Seventeen months later, on September 30, 1897, she died at the age of twenty-four.

Thérèse has been called "the greatest saint of modern times," a designation bestowed on her by Pius XI and since taken up by millions of devotees. What did she do, in those nine years in the monastery, to earn this acclamation? On the surface of things, next to nothing, apart from writing her autobiography on the orders of her Mother Superior. For Thérèse sought God not in grand cataclysms, but in the smallest of events (folding laundry, polishing the silverware) and in the absence of events, the silences that fill the interstices of our lives. Here, we hearken back to Brother Lawrence's practice of the presence. We have come full circle. But the circle proves to be a spiral, for Thérèse carries us one step further along the path toward God. In her "little way," we find the continual awareness of God's presence expressed in a new, more radical mode. Thérèse makes explicit what lies implicit in Brother Lawrence's method and in all Christian practice: utter abandonment to love. She wrote many passages proclaiming her surrender to love, but none more fervent than these in her June 9, 1895, "Act of Oblation to Merciful Love," addressed directly to God:

> In order to live in one single act of perfect Love, I offer myself as a victim of holocaust to your merciful love, asking You to consume me incessantly, allowing the waves of infinite tenderness

shut up within You to overflow into my soul. . . . I want, O my Beloved, at each beat of my heart to renew this offering to You an infinite number of times . . . [3]

Underneath this purple passion lies a revolutionary truth, expressed in Thérèse's promise to renew her love "at each beat of my heart." According to Thérèse, true love—and the true *conversio* that leads to it—doesn't demand spectacular public sacrifice (as in the literal holocaust that consumed St. Joan of Arc, whose death at the stake Thérèse portrayed in a monastery play). It may simply require putting the forks, knives, and spoons away in their proper order. As an adolescent, Thérèse dreamed of a Joan-like martyrdom; genuine *conversio,* she discovered as an adult, lay in sweeping away these fantasies and turning instead to the plain, hard work of sweeping the convent floors. At "each beat of [the] heart," Thérèse teaches, by attending faithfully to the task before us, we can turn from self-will toward the will of God. In this process lie the root, trunk, and branch of real humility, real maturity, real *conversio.*

So far on this retreat, we have shied away from any consideration of morality. This caution makes sense, for moral discussion can easily degenerate into carping, knuckle-rapping, or bombast. I have neither the wish nor the expertise to write guidelines for the moral life; God did the job rather well in sacred scripture. However, no presentation of *conversio* can afford to skip the issue entirely, for spiritual transformation never takes place in a void, but in a landscape of moral decisions for good or evil that affect not only ourselves but others, near and far. In the last analysis, the depth of our *conversio* may depend on how we respond to moral choices.

Bearing these considerations in mind, I suggest that we leap over specific issues and instead explore the source of all moral decisions, that mysterious presence that we commonly call "conscience." Few people agree on what conscience is, or how it comes to prick us with such gusto; nonetheless, we all know it when we feel it—that inner prod that tells us, often in the face of burning desire, to do this or to refrain from doing that. Conscience seems to be an organ, like eyes or ears, that part of oneself that perceives good and evil and that guides one toward the good. Something of God dwells in conscience. We may call it a whisper from heaven, or God's yeast at work in the world.

Whatever metaphor we choose to describe conscience, we all know the difficulties of listening and responding to its promptings (here again, we find "to listen" and "to do": by following conscience, we wed yesterday's promise of obedience to today's of *conversio*). Certainly, our task demands more than just adherence to local codes of behavior, which may sanction activities—say, cannibalism or infanticide—that cut our conscience badly. Nor, as I think we all recognize, can we simply do whatever feels good. Neither gluttony nor passivity will lead us to conscience. Once again, St. Benedict's principle of moderation lights the way. To know our conscience, we must cultivate a mature relationship to our desires. The body's ceaseless clamorings—for sex, for sleep, for food—need to be kept in check, lest we perish like those laboratory rats who, offered unlimited quantities of sugar, eat until they burst. We need to harness our carnal appetites to our higher hunger for health, love, and union with God. If we do so, eventually a new voice sounds within us, that of the awakened conscience: faint and frail at first, so tiny a thing that we see how exactly right Walt Disney was to personify it as a cricket. Only gradually, by fits and starts, do we become able to follow Jiminy Cricket's counsel to "let your conscience be your guide."

As an experiment in *conversio,* including its moral dimension, I would like to propose that you draw up a list of everything that you wish to change about yourself. Your catalog should include physical improvements, such as losing weight or building up stamina; mental improvements, like learning Japanese or reading Homer; and moral improvements, such as corking your temper or your inclination to belittle others. Once you have completed your list, select one item—*only one*—on which to work. Choose something important (not, say, to find a better hair rinse) and something doable (not, for instance, to be free from anger at all times). From now on, this becomes your goal. Make it the center of your life. Work on it every day, without fail. Please be patient with this task. Whatever your goal, almost certainly you will backslide more than once. No matter: God's patience will outlast your own. You will soon discover that your ambition has become the flagship for a flotilla of other longed-for changes in your life. Combat of this sort enhances rather than depletes our inner strength; once we tackle one resolution, we find the power to wrestle with the next. This process, whereby one virtue imparts life to another, may help us to grasp the wisdom in Jesus' demand, so terrifying at first glance, to "be perfect, therefore, as your heavenly Father is perfect" (Matthew 5:48). All *conversio* tends toward perfection. That we will never attain this state doesn't matter—or rather, it matters more than anything, for it means that we always have a goal toward which to strive.

TODAY'S PRAYER THEMES: ADORATION AND PRAISE

What do we mean by adoration, the first of our two intertwined prayer themes? It derives from *adorare*, Latin for "to pray to," an embellishment of *orare*, "to speak." Adoration is thus intimately linked to speech, the fundamental act by which we go beyond ourselves to meet the world. Witness that glorious moment in the 1962 film *The Miracle Worker* when little

Helen Keller—locked since infancy in the solitary confinement of her own body, with iron bars across her eyes, ears, and mouth—discovers the miracle of language while running her fingers under a gushing pump. Suddenly, the prison walls collapse, the world rushes in, and speech is born for this suffering child. Few more ecstatic moments exist in world cinema. None evoke more forcefully the impulse of prayer. We rejoice with Helen in the discovery that language carries meaning, that words unite us with all creation, that language is an act of love. With Helen, we instinctively turn to God in adoration, responding to what she describes in *My Religion* as "the Lord's constant, loving invitation through His Word to all of us, to come Unto Him and choose life."[4]

Orare, adorare: All humans speak and all humans pray (even our earliest ancestors, judging by the ritual substances unearthed at Pleistocene burial sites, sought forms of communication with the supermundane). The world's oldest poems, the Vedic hymns, sing of the majesty of the gods, among them Vac, the goddess of speech. You might recall, too, that *adorare* means not just "to pray," but "to pray to," to pray toward something—or Someone. Speech and song culminate in prayer, and prayer culminates by turning our face in adoration toward God. And just as speech implies knowledge—a grasp, however tentative, of the meaning embedded in words—so does adoration depend on knowledge of God. Coleridge wrote that "in wonder all philosophy began; in wonder it ends. . . . but the first wonder is the offspring of ignorance; the last is the parent of adoration." The prayer of adoration, then, includes more than raw amazement at the world (Coleridge's "first wonder"); it includes conscious reflection on God's many splendors.

To understand adoration better, and to grasp its implications for our retreat, consider the following poem by George

Herbert, whose verses on prayer epitomized the first day of our retreat:

> Come, my Way, my Truth, my Life:
> Such a Way as gives us breath:
> Such a Truth as ends all strife:
> Such a Life as killeth death.
>
> Come, my Light, my Feast, my Strength:
> Such a Light, as shows a feast:
> Such a Feast, as mends in length:
> Such a Strength, as makes his guest.
>
> Come my Joy, my Love, my Heart:
> Such a Joy, as none can move:
> Such a Love, as none can part:
> Such a Heart, as joys in love.

In this wonderful hymn of adoration, Herbert rejoices in God by calling upon nine divine names: Way, Truth, Life, Light, Feast, Strength, Joy, Love, Heart. These nine fall neatly into three triads, to each of which Herbert devotes a stanza. The first stanza speaks of Way, Truth, and Life, qualities that define God's sacred being. The second celebrates Light, Feast, and Strength, qualities that define God's glory. The third sings of Joy, Love, and Heart, qualities that define God's goodness.

Goodness, glory, sacred being: together, these terms suggest—they can never encompass—the nature of God. As we mull them over, we may notice something remarkable: These things seem to have some connection to our own human attributes of mind, body, and heart. In this threefold description of God we see ourselves, perfected (Truth as perfection of mind, Strength as perfection of body, Love as perfection of heart). Perhaps we begin to understand that startling, almost scandalous teaching, that human beings have been created in the image and likeness of God. We adore, then, because in God we find ourselves and in ourselves we find God. At the heart of adoration, no less than of *conversio,* lies the mystery of love, which binds us to one another and to God: "God is love, and those who abide in love abide in God, and God abides in them" (1 John 4:16).

Adoration ranks as the highest monastic activity, the final aim of *opus Dei, lectio divina,* and manual labor. Of course, we can't segregate adoration from other prayer modes like thanksgiving and petition. Love inspires all. We give thanks for God's love; we petition through trust in God's love; we praise God as the source of love. Nonetheless, adoration marks a new stage in the life of prayer, a step forward in the monastic way that we tread on this retreat. For just as children mature by learning to recognize the world in its own right rather than simply in reference to themselves, just so in adoration we reveal our spiritual maturity by shifting our focus from ourselves onto God. In adoration, then, we marvel, rejoice, glory, bless, stand in acclamation, kneel in amazement, bow in humbleness before God without reservation or restraint.

Adoration is intimately linked to praise, the second of today's two prayer themes. We *adore* God as God, the ineffable I AM WHO I AM of Exodus. We *praise* God for the gifts of creation, for man and woman, spider and robin, sun and moon, whirlwind and watery abyss, the great chain of being unrolled in Genesis. We *praise* creation, both for its intrinsic beauty and goodness, and as a palpable sign of God's skillful hand. To those with eyes to see, all creation bears the watermark of God, as William Blake discloses in the conclusion of *A Vision of the Last Judgment:*

> "What," it will be Question'd, "When the Sun rises, do you not see a round disk of fire somewhat like a Guinea?" "O no, no, I see an Innumerable company of the Heavenly host crying 'Holy, Holy, Holy is the Lord God Almighty.' I question not my Cor-

poreal or Vegetative Eye any more than I would Question a Window concerning a Sight. I look thro' it & not with it."

How may we adore and praise on this third day of our retreat? Let us ascend a four-runged ladder, passing through praise of people, crafts, and nature, to climax in adoration of the Source of all that was, is, or ever will be:

People: Let us praise those whom we love, who staunch our wounds, suffer our stupidities, and champion our cause. Call each beloved to mind as vividly as you can. Praise him, praise her! Praise her small charms, her great gifts, her love for you. What does her presence bring to life in you? How will you greet her when you meet her again? Praise God, in whom all of us "live and move and have our being" (Acts 17:28). Here we discover the indissoluble tie between God and people, for how can I love my beloved (as is commonly said, how can I "adore" her) without loving and adoring the God who made her and sustains her? We glimpse, too, the moral force of praise. For in my beloved, I see all human beings. In her dignity, I find my own, and I remember the high state to which I am called. Through praise of others, *conversio* is born.

Art and Artifacts: Let us praise the work of our hands. J. R. R. Tolkien, who knew whereof he spoke, believed that the artist or artisan functions as a "subcreation" whose activities reflect—in a glass, darkly—God's own creation ex nihilo. Something of God flows in our veins, and gives life to our arts and artifacts. Not all created things evoke praise, of course; always, moral considerations apply (for who would praise an executioner's axe?) But if something displays both intrinsic beauty and a noble purpose, we can be sure that it mirrors the goodness of God.

Almost all common tools fulfill this definition. Examine a basic utilitarian device: a fork, a hammer, a pencil. Imagine its history—how that hammer began as soil, sun, and air, its head refined from a lump of iron, its handle cut from a hardwood tree. Trace its evolution; bring to mind the innumerable people—miners, farmers, factory workers, sales clerks—who delivered that hammer into your hands. Each of these people has a story to tell, an epic tale that has taken a lifetime to write. Praise them! Think of all the people united to these hammer-makers, as father or mother, sister or brother, cousin, friend, enemy. What better evidence of the interconnectedness of all creation? Praise them all! Turn then to the hammer's ingenious design, to its perfect balance, its appropriate weight (heavy enough to drive a nail, light enough to lift) and shape (front flat for hammering, back split for wrenching). No wonder Thor, mightiest of Norse gods, chose as his emblem the lowly hammer. Praise it!

Let us turn, then, from artifacts to art. If you brought a holy icon with you on retreat, study it now. If not, find a picture on the wall or in a book or (last resort) in memory, that speaks of God. Scrutinize its color, composition, content. Imagine the artist who stood in front of it; praise him! Savor the painting's beauty, in which you catch a glimpse of the beauty of God, Maker of its maker. "We have Art that we may not perish from Truth," said Nietzsche; the beauty of subcreation, no less than the beauty of Creation, reveals the presence of God. Praise all beauty!

Nature: Let us praise the natural world. Nature has been compared often to a veil or a mask, cloaking the Divine Face. I would like to exchange this image for another, a contemporary metaphor that emphasizes nature's transparency rather than its opacity: Let us imagine the world as a photographic slide, of infinite extension and immeasurable age, through which passes the light of God. Now, we see a slide by virtue of the light that shines through it, and we see the light by virtue of the images it reveals. Just so, we experience God's light as it shines through the world, and we see the world through the shining of God's light.

How can we be alive to this sense of nature as theophany, the visible presence of God? Sometimes this awareness takes us by surprise: We are rocking in a hammock, adrift in daydreams, when without warning a nuthatch swoops down to snatch a bright red berry from a holly bush, and suddenly we see in that bird, that berry, that glorious swoop, the signature of God. But this appreciation of nature as drenched in God's presence needn't seize us unaware. We can cultivate this faculty. Here, St. Francis can be our tutor: For through his humility and openness to all, Francis became a brother to all sentient beings. Wolves behaved like puppies by his side; birds ceased their fluttering to listen to his homilies. Anyone who spends much time in the company of animals knows how warmly they respond to human affection: What then of their response to a saint as advanced as Francis, to a human love that has become, through a lifetime of *conversio,* a transparency through which shines God's own love?

It's reasonable to assume that none of us will attain Francis's degree of sanctity, but we can all learn from his example to be more sensitive to God's presence in nature. Walk outside, in garden or woods or along a stream. Pick a pleasant spot, settle down, and examine your surroundings. Consider only a small region, perhaps no more than ten feet square. What do you find here? You may discover your little empire to be crawling with life—arachnids, beetles, worms, or larger mammalian forms like squirrels, mice, voles. Rocks, plants, fungi, soil also crowd the scene. Don't forget to look up, into the shaft of air that rises from your tiny plot of land to outer space. What extraordinary airborne beasts, what devious currents of wind, what exotic spores and pollens it contains. Nor should you forget to look down, deep beneath the soil's surface; let your imagination sink, like Jules Verne's intrepid explorers, to the center of the earth.

Now that you have a grasp, however frail, of the staggering intricacies within this snip of territory, choose one aspect of it to meditate upon at length: a dung beetle clambering over a hummock, a rock glistening with mica, a half-crushed daisy. Study this thing that God has made. Sentient or not, it remains a marvel. Befriend it, learn its complexities. Let us suppose that you have chosen a patch of heather. Narrow your attention to one square inch of it: See how its colors shimmer, break, and coalesce over each millimeter of surface, see how the life pulses within it. Learn it, stalk by stalk. Praise it! This exercise gives rise to wonder, and this "wonder born of knowledge" gives birth, as Coleridge says, to adoration.

God: Let us praise and adore God. All leads to God, for all comes from God. Sun and moon, snails and slugs, our ability to differentiate snails and slugs, our sense of truth, of right, of beauty, all stem from God. According to the Christian tradition, life's real aim—no matter how avidly we disguise it or deny it with noisy diversions—is to find, know, and unite with God. Praise for people, for craft, for art, for nature, all come to completion in praise of God. The sign of this, St. Isaac of Syria tells us, is that

> A man's heart burns for all creation—men, birds, animals, demons, and all creatures. . . . Great and powerful compassion fills a man's heart . . . so that he cannot endure, hear or see any harm or the least pain suffered by a creature. This is why he prays hourly [for] . . . creation . . . with a great compassion which wells up in his heart without measure until he become likened in this to God.[5]

To "become likened in this to God," writes Isaac. What a remarkable idea, to be like God. Yet this extravagant ambition, smacking of hubris, has always been the goal of monasticism and, indeed, of all Christian life. Notice, however, that Isaac qualifies his declaration: We are likened to God in the "great compassion that wells up in our heart without measure." In compassion, in love, in these very human qualities, we find our kinship to God.

Here we must turn to the example of Christ, whom Christianity acclaims as both God and man. To whatever degree we "conform ourself to Christ," as the ancient formula has it, to that extent we follow Isaac's advice to become "likened to God." We arrive at last at the fundamental monastic practice, the struggle to be like Christ, to "put on Christ," as Paul puts it, so that "the life of Jesus may be made visible in our mortal flesh" (2 Corinthians 4:11). In this idea of conformity to Christ, we find the supreme union of our two themes for today, adoration and *conversio*. For through the process of continual *conversio*, we become likened to that which we adore; we find in ourselves something of the perfect humanity and perfect divinity of Jesus. In rare cases, teach the saints, this process culminates in "divinization" or "deification," the total transformation of the human person through union with God. "Those who participate in Him," wrote St. Gregory Palamas, the fourteenth-century exponent of hesychasm (the movement which, you will remember, gave birth to the Jesus Prayer), "will live in a godlike manner, having attained a divine and heavenly form of life."[6]

But what does this lofty teaching mean to us, who are neither monks nor nuns nor saints of any stripe, who struggle every day just to like our friends, much less love our enemies? Does this extraordinary idea have any practical value on our retreat? Indeed it does. Deification can serve us as both goad and goal, for it is, in fact, the concrete expression of that perfection that Jesus counseled. Even now, as we slog through the trenches, we can work toward conformity with Christ. In his impeccable life we find, written in flesh and blood, a reliable road map to perfection. For this reason, if for no other, we read the New Testament while on monastic retreat. The daily suggestions for *lectio divina,* the scriptural passages peppered throughout this book, our private rambles through the gospels, all point us toward Christ's life as a model for our own.

In his brief life—of which we possess so few fragments—one activity recurs again and again, so often that it can be called the dominant note against which all others sound: Jesus molds his will to that of the One who sent him—"Not my will but yours be done" (Luke 22:42). His commitment is total; Jesus speaks these words in Gethsemane, in his hour of betrayal, when to champion his own will might have meant escape from crucifixion, perhaps even a long life capped by a distinguished old age. But Jesus surrenders all to God, in an intimacy so great that only the mysterious designations of "Father" and "Son" suffice to describe it:

> Very truly, I tell you, the Son can do nothing on his own, but only what he sees the Father doing; for whatever the Father does, the Son does likewise. . . . As I hear, I judge; and my judgment is just, because I seek to do not my own will but the will of him who sent me. *(John* 5:19, *30)*

If, in our work toward *conversio* on this retreat—and during the rest of our lives—deification serves us as goal, Jesus as teacher, and his life as model, may surrender to God's will serve as our method. In doing so, we join hands with every monk and nun in the world. For, as said above, searching out God's will is the final aim of monastic vocation. Monks and nuns want nothing more than to love; as Father Anselm explained, "the will of God is other people." We celebrate in this great endeavor the final marriage of all the acts and themes of our retreat: of thanksgiving, petition, and adoration; of stability, obedience, and *conversio;* of death, gestation, and resurrection.

"Do not be foolish, but understand what the will of the Lord is," says Paul (Ephesians 5:17), for in so doing we find our bliss: "For this is the will of God, your sanctification" (1 Thessalonians 4:3).

PRAYER PRACTICE FOR SUNDAY

For twenty centuries, a single prayer has remained at the center of all monastic practice: the Lord's Prayer, delivered by Jesus to his disciples when they asked him, "Lord, teach us to pray." Even today, it remains the best-known prayer in the world. The customary formulation goes like this:

> Our Father who art in heaven,
>   hallowed be thy name.
> Thy kingdom come, thy will be done,
>   on earth as it is in heaven.
> Give us this day our daily bread,
>   and forgive us our trespasses,
>   as we forgive those who trespass against us.
> And lead us not into temptation,
>   but deliver us from evil.

In this prayer we discern in primordial form all of Jesus' most fundamental teachings, among them the primacy of love over hate, forgiveness over vindictiveness, and above all, the summons to unite our will to that of God ("thy will be done on earth as it is in heaven"). In addition, the Lord's Prayer establishes our intimate, even familial, relationship to God ("our Father"), proclaims God's holiness ("hallowed be thy name"), petitions God ("give us this day our daily bread," signifying, of course, not only baked grains but also the spiritual nutriment, the *manna,* that we need to feed our souls), and humbly asks God to forgive our faults in light of our forgiveness to others, the reciprocity essential to all real relationship ("forgive us our trespasses, as we forgive those who trespass against us"). In sum, the Lord's Prayer, no less than the Jesus Prayer, epitomizes the entire teaching of Christ.

On this last day of our retreat, I suggest that we recite the Lord's Prayer silently at regular intervals, just as we did with the Jesus Prayer. We will find significant differences between the two prayers. The Lord's Prayer, because of its greater length and complexity, has none of the mantra-like qualities of the Jesus Prayer. It demands a different kind of attention, more fluid, more alert to changes in content. Its life inside us will vary accordingly. Let us be sure to listen to each word, to dwell as long as possible on each phrase, each sentence, to soak ourselves in the prayer's liquid rhythms, its stately beauty. At first we will find ourselves drawn to one aspect of the prayer—perhaps the plea for forgiveness, or the call to do God's will—depending on our interior state. Later in the day, another phrase will captivate us. Sometimes we will find ourselves wrestling with the nuances of a particular word (what did Jesus mean, after all, by "Father"?); at other times, we will be dazzled by God's mystery, evoked in the phrase "hallowed be thy name"; a little while more, and all parts will unite into a luminous whole, and we will say the prayer as if with a single breath. All this is as it should be, for the Lord's Prayer encompasses all prayer, as God encompasses all creation. The blessings of this prayer cannot be numbered.

A few among us have yet another reason to say the Lord's Prayer, one that might dumbfound them: for the difficulties that it brings. Allow me to explain. Some people object to all traditional prayer. Why, they ask, don't we compose our own prayers in a contemporary idiom? Why speak of "kingdom" when we inhabit a democracy? Others object to the prayer's use of "Father." Isn't this title a vestige of discarded social views? Others feel bewildered by the plea that God "lead us not into temptation." How can this God that tempts, so reminiscent of the serpent in Eden or the devil that assails Jesus in the wilderness, at the same time be the God of love?

Rather then respond to each of these objections in turn—a task that would require a guided tour through the subtleties of biblical translation, Trinitarian theology, philology, traditionalism, and more—I'd like to lift our discussion to another plane entirely. I ask you to call to mind the monastic attitude that we have tried to cultivate on this retreat, a posture of patience, humbleness, and love. I'll never forget the words that an elderly nun, long experienced in the religious life, addressed to me many years ago in response to my caustic comment about a friend's moral dereliction. She gazed at me kindly for a moment and then said, "In the monastery, we are trained never to judge."

I am still struggling to plumb the depths of her advice. Nothing cuts against the grain more fiercely, for we judge everything, all the time: the weather, politicians, last night's movie, our lover's face, the thickness of our sandwich. Not to judge! If we could put into practice this wonderful principle, I've little doubt that it would transform the world. But a host of banshees block our way, and the worst of them is habit. Let us pit ourselves against our habits, our reactions, our arrogant certainties. The rewards we reap will be immediate and lasting. Why go on retreat, if not to confront our biases, the easy likes and dislikes that rule our lives, and to discover instead new ways of seeing and doing? Right here, right now, a few of us have a splendid opportunity to quell our ego, to combat our self-love. I especially urge those with a resistance to the Lord's Prayer to make it their prayer practice for the third day of our retreat.

FINISHING THE DAY

As Sunday draws to a close, we continue the pattern of previous days: another half hour of contemplation, followed by Compline, listening to music, writing in our journal. We should leave this last evening of retreat free of all busy work, so that the cumulative effect of three days of solitude can begin to settle into our inmost beings. Some of us might want to say a special prayer tonight to our chosen saint, asking for guidance and grit as we prepare to rejoin the world (the transition back to ordinary life will be discussed in chapter 7).

To finish the day, I suggest that we meditate on the following poem by the great Jesuit writer Gerard Manley Hopkins (1844–89), which incorporates so many of the themes (praise, *conversio*, resurrection) that we explored today:

GOD'S GRANDEUR

The world is charged with the grandeur of God.
    It will flame out, like shining from shook foil;
    It gathers to a greatness, like the ooze of oil
Crushed. Why do men then now not reck his rod?
Generations have trod, have trod, have trod;
    And all is seared with trade; bleared, smeared with toil;
    And wears man's smudge and shares man's smell: the soil
Is bare now, nor can foot feel, being shod.

And for all this, nature is never spent;
    There lives the deepest freshness deep down things;
And though the last lights off the black West went
    Oh, morning, at the brown brink eastward, springs—
Because the Holy Ghost over the bent
    World broods with warm breast and with ah! bright wings.

Chapter Seven

ENDS
AND
BEGINNINGS

I'll never forget my first return to the world following a retreat. My solitude had lasted a scant five days, yet when I quit my refuge—a dilapidated shack edging its way down a slope on the Vermont–Massachusetts border—I felt like Robinson Crusoe sailing away from his island hideaway after twenty-eight years of exile. As I sauntered toward my car, I drank in the sensations that rushed my way—a horse's whinny from a faraway field, a girl in a blue velvet dress spinning a yellow hoop, the rank odor of hay rotting in a rick. Everything trembled with inner light, God seemed woven into the landscape, the sky, the very air.

The first shock came ten minutes later, when I reached the nearest town and suddenly found myself in a fractured jigsaw puzzle of clashing colors, screeching cars, stench and glare, jostling crowds. I felt dizzy, confused, badly dislocated—all this, mind you, in a village of less than 5,000 souls. For relief I dashed into a nearby supermarket, only to discover there the ninth circle of Hell: row upon row of cans, crates, boxes, bags, bushels, barrels, filled with contents bright and bumpy, wrapped in acres of cardboard, square miles of plastic, a glut beyond imagining—the sanctum sanctorum of American consumerism—and every inch plastered with slogans that screamed for attention. My head swam.

Just then a voice called out my name ("God called to him out of the burning bush"). I turned around and saw a dear friend approach. She hugged me, elated at our meeting. Her sweet greeting unlocked my heart. I knew then what St. Benedict meant when he said that "all guests who present themselves are to be welcomed as Christ . . . because he is indeed welcomed in them" (*RB* 53). For I saw in my friend the likeness of the God whom I had sought, prayed to, wept over, befriended during my solitude. I needn't have feared: God had come with me out of the retreat.

Shock will be our inevitable companion as we return to the world, at least during our first years of spiritual practice. We can be ready to meet it by planting our feet firmly in God. Grip onto the Lord's Prayer, the Jesus Prayer, or Brother Lawrence's practice of the presence; any of these will help to bring stability and strength. Remember St. Antony emerging from twenty years of solitude: "He maintained utter equilibrium, like one guided by reason and steadfast in that which accords with nature." Perhaps we can't claim this high state as our own, but we too have entered on the path to equilibrium. For a few days, we have felt the rough, satisfying scratch of the monastic habit against our skins. We have worn it lightly and fleetingly, as befits ordinary men and women on brief monastic retreat. Now we must learn how to wear it in the world.

In this effort, we have a decent head start. We now enjoy a beginner's acquaintance with contemplation. We know how prayer can sanctify our day. We have tasted the monastic routines of *opus Dei, lectio divina,* and manual labor, and the monastic promises of stability, obedience, and *conversio*. Our job becomes that of safeguarding these riches from the tarnish of neglect. In order to maintain their luster in our hearts, we must polish them daily, as St. Francis de Sales advises:

> As the birds have nests on the trees that they may have a retreat when they need it . . . so our hearts ought to seek out and choose some place each day . . . near to our Lord, that they may make their retreat on all occasions.[1]

We may well be daunted by this challenge. How do we sustain retreat in the midst of the world's hot pawings, not to mention its indifference to the inner life? As a start, I ask you to determine which of the many monastic practices covered in this book suit you best. Lock them into your heart. Return to them unflaggingly. Don't let a day go by without some form of prayer. As Kierkegaard reminds us, "Prayer does not change God, but it changes him who prays." Be ready, whenever you hear the call, to plunge within yourself—whether driving or eating or negotiating a deal—and there offer thanks, petitions, and praise to God. In this gesture we see the true meaning of retreat: not only physical withdrawal from the world (although it is that, to be sure), but an interior disposition grounded in love. As we have learned by now, this inner opening to God can take place in the midst of daily work. "Rejoice always, pray without ceasing, give thanks in all circumstances," writes Paul, "for this is the will of God in Christ Jesus for you" (1 Thessalonians 5:16–18).

A special opportunity beckons those who wish a stronger connection to monastic life. Through Benedictine oblation, we may forge an official (but pliable) bond with a monastery of our choosing. The word "oblation" derives from the Latin *oblatio*, "offering"; by making our oblation, we offer ourselves in service to God and the world. As I mentioned in chapter 2, oblates come from many different denominations—or none at all. The only prerequisite is a desire to live according to the precepts laid down in the *Rule* of St. Benedict, insofar as circumstances permit.

Benedictines belong to a worldwide community, or "Order" (thus the initials O.S.B., "Order of St. Benedict," always written after the name of professed monks and nuns). Nonetheless, each monastery remains a self-sufficient, self-governing entity, with its own particular Benedictine flavor. Oblation is made to the individual monastery rather than to the Order at large. It's wise, therefore, to scout out a number of monasteries before settling on one for oblation. In the United States, Benedictine communities run the gamut from traditional houses whose members wear full habit, chant in Latin, and encourage contemplative prayer, to houses that operate private schools or universities and sing the Divine Office in English accompanied by folk guitar. My taste runs toward the richness of tradition, yours may not. Whatever your inclinations, there will be a monastery for you.

What rewards does oblation bring? Above all, membership in a monastic family, with whom one unites in love of God. By accepting apprenticeship under Benedict's rule, the oblate finds available in his or her daily life, with the support of the monastery, some share in the many spiritual treasures sketched in this book. Some monasteries appoint, from among senior monks or nuns, an oblate director who may dispense spiritual advice upon request. Many houses sponsor annual retreat days; some publish an oblate newsletter, often an amateurish affair whose surface shortcomings only highlight by contrast the holiness to be found within.

As this book goes to press, no central clearinghouse exists for information on Benedictine oblation. To obtain the location of the nearest Benedictine monastery, you might contact your local Catholic, Episcopal, or Lutheran church, or—as improbable as it sounds—check the Yellow Pages.

What can we say in conclusion about our retreat? Most likely, none of us heard the heavenly hosts shouting hosannah, or spied fiery chariots streaking across the sky, or felt his heart ignite with the strange mystical fire of which the hesychasts write. On the whole, God reserves such gifts for other people. What then came our way? For a few days, we left behind our customary activities, we prayed, we read, we worked with our hands. We may not have stormed the land of milk and honey, but perhaps we glimpsed what lies around the next bend in the lifelong path that winds from us to God.

Or perhaps not. Perhaps we learned only to put one foot in front of another, or achieved no more than to catch our breath before one day—next week? next year?—taking our first real step. Rest assured: This is no mean accomplishment. God rushes to answer our smallest efforts, as Jesus taught: "Ask, and it will be given you; search, and you will find; knock, and the door will be opened for you." In this lovely triple pledge, Jesus assures us of God's courtesy toward all creatures. His promise lead us directly to the final theme and the final exercise of our retreat.

If the Divine Office is the monastic prayer par excellence, hospitality holds high court among monastic virtues. The Benedictine prepares a place apart—and then opens the door to all who knock. As we have seen, Benedict asks his monks to turn away no one, to welcome everyone as Christ. This gracious activity can be ours as well. The secret of hospitality lies, I believe, in the ability to recognize beauty whenever we meet it. Mother Teresa of Calcutta describes her work, which includes plucking maggots from the ulcerating limbs of the homeless and dying, as "something beautiful for God." What imparts beauty to her work, she says, is the beauty of those whom she helps. In her eyes, these faces ravaged by disease, poverty, or violence remain luminous with the presence of God. From this beauty she draws the strength for her impossible task, answering knocks and opening doors on behalf of the "poorest of the poor" twenty-four hours a day.

Beauty works its magic whenever we recognize its knock and let it in. It resurrects us, gives us hope, awakens us to truth, opens us to love. Hospitality is most beautiful, and beauty most hospitable. Let us leave our retreat, then, with a vow of hospitality. Let us welcome whatever comes our way—a dying friend, a reclusive spider, a jewel-encrusted icon, the apothegms of Christ—and find in these gifts the beauty of all created things and of our God, who breathes them into being and upholds them through love.

Notes

Chapter 1

1. Julian of Norwich, *Showings*, translated by Edmund Colledge, O.S.A., and James Walsh, S.J. (New York: Paulist Press, 1978), 130.
2. Robert Bretall, *A Kierkegaard Anthology* (Princeton, NJ: Princeton University Press, 1946), 150.
3. Anthanasius, *The Life of Antony*, translated by Robert C. Gregg (New York: Paulist Press, 1980), 42.
4. Saint Augustine, *Confessions*, translated by R. S. Pine-Coffin (London: Penguin Books, 1961), 197.

Chapter 2

1. Wallace Shawn and Andre Gregory, *My Dinner with Andre* (New York: Grove Press, 1981), 95.
2. Denis Huerre, O.S.B., *Letters to My Brothers and Sisters*, translated by Sylvester Houédard, O.S.B. (Collegeville, MN: The Liturgical Press, 1994), 22.
3. "The Sayings of the Desert Fathers," in Owen Chadwick, *Western Asceticism* (Philadelphia: Westminster Press, 1958), 150.
4. Pope Saint Gregory the Great, *Life and Miracles of St. Benedict*, translated by Odo J. Zimmermann, O.S.B., and Benedict R. Avery, O.S.B. (Collegeville, MN: The Liturgical Press, no date), 12.
5. Huerre, *Letters to My Brothers and Sisters*, 22.

Chapter 4

1. Jacques Lusseyran, *And There Was Light*, translated by Elizabeth R. Cameron (Boston: Little, Brown, and Co., 1963; reprint ed., New York: Parabola Books, 1987), 14.

2. Lusseyran, *And There Was Light,* 16.
3. Lusseyran, *And There Was Light,* 16–17.
4. Lusseyran, *And There Was Light,* 27.
5. Lusseyran, *And There Was Light,* 281–83.
6. Lusseyran, *And There Was Light,* 29.
7. Brother Lawrence of the Resurrection, *Writings and Conversations on the Practice of the Presence of God,* Critical Edition by Conrad De Meester, O.C.D., translated by Salvatore Sciurba, O.C.D. (Washington, DC: ICS Publications, 1994), 36.

Chapter 5

1. Jacques Lusseyran, *And There Was Light,* translated by Elizabeth R. Cameron (Boston: Little, Brown, and Co., 1963; reprint ed., New York: Parabola Books, 1987), 46–47.
2. For scientific findings on the efficacy of prayer, see Larry Dossey, *Healing Words: The Power of Prayer and the Practice of Medicine* (San Francisco: HarperSanFrancisco, 1991).
3. Anonymous, *The Way of a Pilgrim,* translated by R. M. French (2nd ed., New York: Harper, 1954; reprint ed., New York: HarperCollins, 1991), 38.
4. Anonymous, *The Way of a Pilgrim,* 39.

Chapter 6

1. Quoted in Esther De Waal, *Seeking God* (Collegeville, MN: The Liturgical Press, 1984), 70.
2. St. Thérèse of Lisieux, *Story of a Soul,* translated by John Clarke, O.C.D. (Washington, DC: ICS Publications, 1975, 1976), 134–35.
3. St. Thérèse of Lisieux, *Story of a Soul,* 277.
4. Helen Keller, *My Religion* (Garden City, NY: Doubleday, Page, & Co., 1927), 151.
5. Quoted in Leonid Ouspensky and Vladimir Lossky, *The Meaning of Icons,* translated by G. E. H. Palmer and E. Kadloubovsky (Crestwood, NY: St. Vladimir's Seminary Press, 1989), 92–93.
6. Quoted in Georgios I. Mantzaridis, *The Deification of Man,* translated by Liadain Sherrard (Crestwood, NY: St. Vladimir's Seminary Press, 1984), 22.

Chapter 7

1. Quoted in John Townroe, "Retreat," in *The Study of Spirituality,* edited by Cheslyn Jones, Geoffrey Wainwright, and Edward Yarnold, S.J. (New York, Oxford: Oxford University Press, 1986), 579.

General Index

Retreat centers, 24–25, 46

Retreat Day One: beginning of, with contemplation, 69–71; and Christian meaning of Friday, 60, 61, 79; Divine Office for, 84–94; finishing, 105–7; orientation to locale on, 73–74; pattern of, 63; prayer practice for, 98–102; prayer theme for, 102–4; promise for, 77–78; sacred reading for, 94–95; template for, 63; theme for, 74–77

Retreat Day Three: beginning of, 137–38; and Christian meaning of Sunday, 60, 61, 137, 146; Divine Office for, 138 45; finishing of, 166; pattern of, 63, 137–45; prayer practice for, 163–65; prayer themes for, 153–63; promise for, 146–53; template for, 63; theme for, 145–46

Retreat Day Two: beginning of, 111; and Christian meaning of Saturday, 60, 61, 111; Divine Office for, 112–18; finishing of, 133–34; pattern of, 63, 111–18; prayer practice for, 130–32; promise for, 122–28; template for, 63; theme for, 119–22

Rule (St. Benedict): on Divine Office, 32, 80; on hospitality, 170; influence of, 29; on obedience, 123; and oblation, 172; origin of, 26, 30–31; on perfection, 77; for retreat, 49–50

Sacred reading (*lectio divina*): in monastic routine, 35–37; for retreat, 37–38, 61; for Retreat Day One, 94–95; for Retreat Day Three, 138; for Retreat Day Two, 112. *See also* Books; Scripture readings

Saint, for retreat: choosing of, 54–58; praying to, 102, 166

St. Joseph's Abbey, 62, 64

Salinger, J. D., 131

Salve Regina, 93–94

Sanctity, practice of, 98–102

Santayana, George, 10

Saturday. *See* Retreat Day Two

Scholastica, Saint, 57

Scripture readings, 36–37; for Retreat Day One, 86, 90, 92; for Retreat Day Three, 141, 143, 145; for Retreat Day Two, 114, 117, 118. *See also* Divine Office; Sacred reading

Security, 45–46

Self-denial, 127–28

Self-examination exercise, 133–34

Shakers, 35

Silent prayer, 86, 90, 93

Simeon Stylites, Saint, 11, 44–45

Singing, 32, 81–82

Sitting: for contemplation, 71–73; tools for, 47–48

Spiritual growth, 12–13, 119–20; exercise for, 120–22

Stability promise, 27; for Retreat Day One, 61, 77–78

Star Wars, 98

Sunday. *See* Retreat Day Three

Thanksgiving, 102–4

Theophany, 159

Thérèse of Lisieux, Saint, 55, 58, 98, 102, 149–51

Thoreau, Henry, 11, 59, 95, 137

Tolkien, J.R.R., 157

Tolstoy, Leo, 56

Trust, 64

Under Siege, 98

Veda, 154

Vespers (Evening Office), 33; for Retreat Day One, 88–91; for Retreat Day Three, 141–43; for Retreat Day Two, 115–17; template for, 79

Vianney, Jean, 98

Vigils, 32

Vocalization, 82, 112

White, Edward, 45

Wilson, Maurice, 43, 45

Zusya, Rabbi, 56

Biblical Index